Kindest regards

D1456988

New Rules for the New World

New Rules for the New World

Cautionary Tales for the New World Manager

EDDIE OBENG

CAPSTONE

Copyright © Eddie Obeng

The right of Eddie Obeng to be identified as
author of this work has been asserted in accordance
with the Copyright, Designs and Patents Act 1988.

This edition published 1997 by
Capstone Publishing Limited
Oxford Centre for Innovation
Mill Street
Oxford OX2 0JX
United Kingdom
Reprinted 1997

All rights reserved. Except for the quotation of short
passages for the purposes of criticism and review, no
part of this publication may be reproduced, stored in
a retrievel system, or transmitted, in any form or by
any means, electronic, mechanical, photocopying,
recording or otherwise, without the prior permission
of the publisher or author.

A CIP catalogue record for this book is available
from the British Library

ISBN 1-900961-15-6

Design and Typesetting by Dexter Haven, London

Printed and bound in Great Britain by
T. J. International Ltd, Padstow, Cornwall

This book is printed on acid-free paper

To

My Muse,

my O&O,

Susan

So tell me, why should I read this book?

Most management books promise success and yet few managers following the recommended check lists attain it. Those who do, often succeed because of their **own** intuition and determination. Most managers now have an intuition about what they are supposed to do to meet 'New World'[1] challenges. This is marvelous. But because few academic and management texts actually distinguish between the 'Old World' and 'New World', they are often left feeling alone. They feel as if they are alone in their personal views of what we know must be done to achieve success in the Real World. As a result, many of us have to summon up great reserves of courage, to do what we've got to do. It appears to us that we must strike out alone along a path not well trodden. We need these vast reserves of courage, conviction and skills in case "something goes wrong" – in truth, something usually does go wrong.

Cautionary Tales is a book about what goes wrong. The path from good (and usually correct) intention to final failure. The route from a great idea like, "Why don't we benchmark against our competitors?" to complete industry failure, (i.e. Queen of the pigs: benchmarking against other organizations who are failing).

It is a book of Tales. Each Tale takes the reader from a Great Idea to Failure. It ends with 'morals', new rules for the New World. Rules which would have prevented the failure. Each tale is an account from the manager to a listening and sometimes questioning mentor called Franck. As you read you will get to know Franck. Franck, who describes himself as an educator, helps the storyteller to explore the events and leads them to the threshold of the new rules. (If you've met Franck in the past you will find him surprisingly reticent and muted and sometimes even helpful and supportive in the tales.)

'So what? So what am I supposed to do about this?' I guess you are thinking. I'm not sure. Over the past three years I have been living an experiment called 'The Virtual Business School'. The experiment had two purposes, firstly to pay the mortgage, skiing holidays and my minimum flying hours per year and secondly to test the ideas in modern management thinking and the ideas put forward by Franck in this book. As a result I can vouch personally for all the conclusions Franck draws in and presents in the second part of the book.

The second part of the narrative is a transcript of a learning event run by Franck for the full group to explain and expand on the Rules. Franck provides descriptions of how to apply the new rules in reality. This provides the transition to implementation in the Real World. He has told me that he is quite happy for you to use his work as the basis for any learning activity you are planning to lead on the New World <i.e. to all educators, trainers and management developers, it's open season but please acknowledge your source!>

The third part is Franck's 'action planning session'; I think he calls this a 'future choice session'. Typical consultant jargon, if you ask me. Designed to induce guilt in even the most conscience-free executive, this section completes the book. You may wish to complete it yourself following the route Franck takes his participants. **My** sincere wish is that this section goads you or compels you into action.

Written as a companion to *Achieving Organisational Magic, All Change!, Putting Strategy to Work* and *Making Re-engineering Happen* by Eddie Obeng, *New Rules for the New World* has a heritage of fun, learning and practicality upon which it builds.

Contents

Preface

Cautionary Tales came to me one afternoon when I discovered that an organization I'd been working with for over two years was about to be involved in a merger. I was really upset. The two year implementation program was going very well. Everything had gone right, almost as planned. We had just about achieved critical mass within the executive team. We were succeeding and taking people's hearts and minds with us, whilst developing a new language and 'New World' view. And now it was all up in the air. It wasn't the first time that I had been involved in a 'textbook' strategy implementation (i.e. everything going right) only to have it all thrown to the winds.

The first experience which sticks in my mind was with a manufacturing company. The company, following good 'Old World' practices of cost minimization worked with minimum batch sizes and cost-plus pricing. As the New World had dawned, these concepts had made the company increasingly uncompetitive. Customers, unhappy with the turn-around times, costs and unpredictability had put increasing pressures on the organization to respond. The business performance at the time was lousy. In fact the interest payments on the amount of money represented by the work in progress were as large as the overall profits. Something had to be done and done fast. I had suggested draining out all inventory and re-aligning the work force. They started work. All was going well until we came to year end. Out of the blue we received an urgent message from the CEO to stop work immediately. It seemed that our work was affecting the share price. Quite simply, by draining out the inventory, at the stock check, the asset base was seen to have been reduced. The reduced work in progress had been interpreted by city analysts as less work in the pipeline, i.e. less secure future cash flows. So the resultant effect of a reduced asset base and uncertain cash projections was a downward pressure on the share price.

I was completely agog <I couldn't think of a more appropriate expression to put here>. We were doing the right thing and yet the measures of our success and performance were encouraging us to do the wrong thing! Even worse they were suggesting that we were failing whilst in fact we were succeeding.

The second influence on me for this book was a survey I read a few years ago. The survey looked at a range of strategy implementation initiatives over the past decade and concluded that only in less than 20% of the cases had the stratagem been successful (i.e. brought back in more money than had been spent). I am a firm believer that 'no-one wakes up on Monday morning planning to get it all wrong and screw everything up' but we get on with living our lives and somehow it does go wrong. I think that the New World environment makes this possibility more likely since we often mix Old and New World ideas unintentionally with devastating results, like in the example above.

I imagined a Canterbury Tales style tome, written in Olde English (or should that be Neuw English?) with stories by different travelers, journeying on the route (or should that be information superhighway?) from the Old World to the New. I also had in mind a book of rhymes for potentially naughty children which was one of my favorites as a child (especially Matilda, who told such dreadful lies it made one gasp and stretch one's eyes and finally came to a sticky end). However, because it is typically difficult to get permission to publish widely case studies about real life corporate cockups <for non-UK read here big mistakes> and failures, I have extracted out the key patterns of the failures and presented them here. So instead of the juicy no-holds-barred in depth exposé you were looking for, instead you have in your hands yet another typically boring and long winded management textbook, (I joke!!) only significantly modified, in line with my values of fun and learning.

In a series of short stories I have tried to highlight the 'New World' mind-set and ideas so that you can recognise them as separate from more traditional ideas. I have never written short stories before so I hope they work for you. The way I normally read books of short stories is to select the sequence to read them in, either by length or by title. I then work my way through them along a convoluted route. You may wish to try reading the first chapter for context and then choosing the story which you feel is most like you. I have written each in the first person which could be a bit confusing since you have to re-calibrate who **you** are after each story. As I did in *All Change!* I have almost completely avoided name dropping or mentioning any major Fortune 500 companies in detailed case studies. Two reasons, firstly, most of them are so large that some part, somewhere is doing something right. Secondly, there is no point in emulating them they probably have more resources than you do and to lead, after all, you must be first, or at least near the front. **All the rules I describe I use myself so I know that they work**. Indeed, five of them are the operating principles of Pentacle The Virtual Business School, and are continuously displayed on our screen saver!

I hope that you find the ideas fun and easy to apply.

Eddie Obeng
Burke Lodge
Beaconsfield
HP9 2JH
UK
44 (0) 1494 678555
eddie_obeng@pentaclethevbs.com

Acknowledgements

Life imitating art.
Art imitating life.

Each of the tales is fictional. The Rules though, are not. I would like to thank the following organisations for helping me discover, learn and understand the new rules for the New World.

Amgen
Bank of Ireland
Boots the Chemist
Pilkingon Ltd
Dera
Glaxo Wellcome UK
ICL
Magnox Electric
Motorola
Nat West Bank
Novartis
Nuclear Electric
Salomon Brothers
SmithKline Beecham
William M Mercer

Also sincere thanks to Richard Bamsey for his wonderful creations, the artwork for the whimsical characters in the tales.

Disclaimer
Although some of the stories appearing here may appear autobiographical, all the events described in this book are entirely fictional. Any resemblance to any person living or dead or any event is merely coincidental.

1

Building Blocks

Building Blocks

A — OLD WORLD/NEW WORLD

Every few hundred years throughout Western History, a sharp transformation has occurred. In a matter of a few decades, society altogether rearranges itself, its world views, its social and political structure, its arts, its key institutions. Fifty years later a New World exists. And the people born into that world cannot even imagine the world in which their grandparents lived and into which their own parents were born.

Peter Drucker

I have a real dilemma. This book is about new rules for the New World. I really want to concentrate on writing about the new rules. I want to concentrate on writing about the new rules rather than writing about the New World. That is the basis of my dilemma. You see, I don't know if you believe in the existence of the New World or really understand all about it. You probably do, or you probably don't. I can't tell. And I don't want to repeat the content of others of my books which spend tens of pages explaining it all, if I can get away with it. Repeating content would mean less value for money for those readers who have already digested the concepts of the New World. It would mean that I was punishing repeat purchases, punishing customer loyalty. Do you see my problem?

What should I do? How about if I suggest that any reader who understands the New World, skips this section and ploughs straight on to page 9? And anyone who doesn't, comes with me on a short exploratory journey into the nature of the New World.

One of my favorite jokes when working with a large group of people is to make a ridiculous assertion and then to tease them about it. I say, "You think it's all roughly the same, but it has all changed. Everything. Gone. Deleted." I then explain with as much sincerity as I can muster, "You see, ten years ago, ten years ago, **at midnight**[2] (usually people laugh at this bit – did you get it?) somebody changed **all** the rules about how to run an organization successfully. Do you remember it happening? (Usually I get stony silence here.) You don't? Well, that's probably because it happened at midnight and you were all asleep. But believe me, it happened." (Some laughter. I know it's not very funny as jokes go, but it's my best).

No-one ever believes that it's all changed. At least most of us wish it hasn't. We wish that, because the thought of throwing out all the things we have taken decades to learn and starting again is much too much. Much too painful. But it **has** changed. If I asked you to tell me what you felt was happening globally in terms of some parameters like the pace of change, complexity of your organization's environment, the level of competition, etc. you would probably say that they had increased. If I asked you about technology, the changes, about the rate at which various technologies are converging and creating new innovations or the rate at which technologies are combined to produce any particular product, service or offering, you would probably reply, now half bored by how obvious you think the answer is, that it had increased. And if I asked you to represent all this graphically, over the past couple of decades, you would probably come up with something like this:

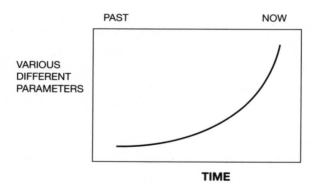

Interesting, but so what? How about if I asked you to think about how fast your organization learns. That is, the time from when it sees something, understands it and knows what to do about it. Take some time to think about this. Note I said your organization, not you, Think about what limits the rate at which your organization learns. Is it the people at the top? Is it the speed or rate at which information about external events, such as customer demand changes, filter into the organisation? What is it? For most people who live in a hierarchy the speed of learning tends to be limited by the people at the top. What about yours?

<Reader to insert one **full** minute of deep thought here>

You have probably concluded that for most organizations a couple of decades ago, the speed of learning was limited by the person (man) at the top. If they were a smart Henry Ford or Thomas Watson Jr., the organization could learn faster than their world changed. If they were not that smart they might get an initial foothold but eventually competition and change would weed them out. We'll only concern ourselves with the smart ones. By smart ones I mean your organization as well. Over the same period what has happened to your organization's ability to learn? Could you represent it graphically on the figure above? The organizations we have decided to consider start with their learning rate higher than the change of the parameters within their local environment. But what happens next? Your go. Fill in your view.

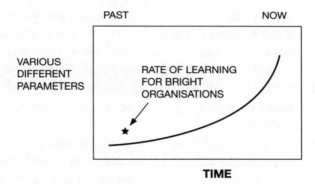

And here's one I made earlier:

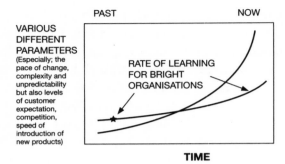

Do you agree? I'm so glad you do. If you didn't I'd have had to have written another ten paragraphs.

So now you are thinking, 'If there is a gap between the two lines the trick is to close the gap.' 'In fact,' you think, 'if only we could close the gap and put the *learning* curve *above* the *'change'* curve we would be in control again. We could run our organization from a position of knowledge.' You have probably concluded that, 'The aim is to learn faster, to create the Learning Organization and then all will be well. We will once again be able to learn faster than the world changes'. 'No!' I exclaim. 'Wrong!'

Why wrong? Because it is now a different context.

Before we move on, I'd like to explain the differences between the two environments. The one in which **you can learn faster** than the world changes versus the one in which **the world changes faster** than you can learn.

If you lived in a world where you could learn faster than the world changed, how would you feel? What would you value? What would the same good rules of thumb be for making money? How would you organize people?

<Reader to insert at least five minutes of deep thought here>

Now, consider what would alter if you lived in a world which could change much faster than you could learn. How would you feel? What would you value? What would the same good rules of thumb be for making money? How would you organize people?

\<This is much tougher, Reader to insert at least seven minutes of deep thought here>

See? They are not the same. In fact, in most instances they are diametrically opposite. And the names, nicknames, I use for these two environments, as if you hadn't guessed, are:

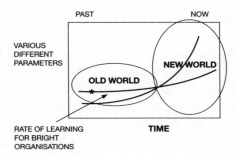

Let me try to explain why the New World is such a nightmare.

Recently, whilst working with a mixed group of managers we began to discuss the nature of the New World. One of the executives said, "We run a factory and we have to replace a major piece of equipment we use for drying our product. In the past we would simply have gone back to a German supplier who was known throughout the industry as the best manufacturer of such furnaces. Now we have a problem. We have discovered that we can obtain a furnace of a similar specification at a fraction of the price from the Far East. And we think that two companies in the US are producing modular units on rental which would provide far more flexibility without the capital investment. But depending on who in the trade you talk to, you get directed towards different offers. And coupled with that, has been the development of microwave driers, which we don't fully understand, nor are we sure of the real benefits we could get from them. We believe that product quality could be improved, perhaps allowing us to raise our prices? How do we make the investment decision? We would take the time to study it but for the fact that the bulk of our time is already taken up with studying our markets and customers. There is no time left to learn all these other things we need to run the business." It is almost as if you must *seek what you do not already know when you do not need it yet.*

Another, an Italian executive topped the first story in a 'mine's bigger than yours' sort of way. He began explaining that their customers and potential customers had so much choice that they couldn't find his company anymore. Because the customers had so little time to evaluate and choose, unless you were lucky enough to be right there, at the front of their minds when they were considering the choice, being the best did not help you to win the order. This meant advertising more at a wider range of potential decision points. But even if they read your advert you also had to help them find an alternative, so that they would feel comfortable in choosing you. He commented that this redefined Service. Service used to be something you offered **after** the decision to purchase from you. Now in the New World *service provision now extends to helping people in their purchase decisions, even if they don't intend to purchase from you!*

Another, a French executive, indicating that the value of experience in the Old World was well and truly gone, and helping me and the others to understand that although you may be able to learn faster in a small area than the world is changing you may be unable to learn faster in the things which you actually need to influence, recounted how as a young boy his father had been able to teach him many things; from how a bicycle worked, to how to mend a car, to how to tie a bow tie. Now he finds with his teenage children that he can teach them nothing. They have an equal chance of working out how a video recorder works and often his son teaches him things, like how to surf the net. The few things he can teach his son are things like personal mastery, focus, compassion and self discipline. It's almost as if in the New World, historical experience and know-how have a shelf life which is short, almost zero. *A significant shelf-life only remains for the knowledge, skills, ideas, values and competences which allow us to influence the future*.

The problem with the New World is not only that we can't learn as fast as the world changes, it is also that many outcomes/outputs, especially for business organizations depend on a wider and wider range of knowledge, skills, values, technologies and competences. This forces us to have to learn about a greater range at a faster speed. The social and government implications of New World are everywhere. Why should Bill Clinton be so concerned over a cloned sheep? Why should a commission be set up to investigate cloning? Only because they were surprised by the news, for years assumed to be science fiction, and for the fact that no one in the government has the faintest clue what effect it is likely to have.

New World creates levels of uncertainty both in our minds and in reality.

That is the problem. Most human beings naturally assume that any change (especially any that they haven't initiated) is a threat to their security. As a result we tend to react emotionally to change. And since most of the people I know are human beings, it means that for most people the *New World creates a persistent, pervading emotionally charged backdrop* to our day-to-day activities. It is against this backdrop that we plan and begin the journey to success into the New World, aware that any changes we begin will often meet with resistance. Not logical resistance but emotional resistance.[3]

B — CYBER CONES

Everything is Nothing! If you go up in scale, you discover that between the unmeasurably small specs of stars, planets and galaxies there is a vastness of Nothing. If on the other hand you go down in scale, you discover that stretching between the unmeasureably small subatomic particles and waves there is a continuum of Nothing. Perhaps it's true. Everything is Nothing!

Do you remember Stephen Hawking's best seller? I think it had 'Time' in the title? Well, I have to confess that I not only bought it, demonstrating what a poser I am, but also read (most of) it. One of the concepts which I found particularly interesting was that of Space-Time. We are used to thinking about Space as three dimensional. Forward-backward; Up-down; side-to-side. But instead of thinking about the dimensions in that way, imagine that they are solid lines. Lines you could fold. So that you could fold them up together, like how you fold away the legs of a camera tripod, just bend each one through 90 degrees until all three legs of the tripod, all three dimensions, were squished into one. Call it 'Space'.

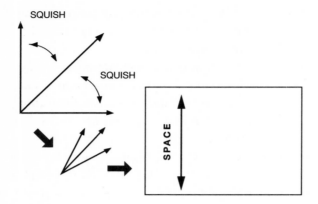

And then recognise that things change from day to day so have another dimension at right angles to Space, called time. So wherever you are in the world and whenever it is, you can be represented by a dot in Space-Time.

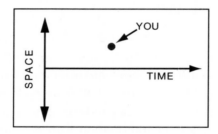

Imagine it was 100 years ago and a young person, called Jed the Inquisitive, was thinking about life and all that they could experience and all they could influence. The speed of travel of a human on the earth (Meatspace/Touchspace[4]) was rather slow and if they really wanted to see the world they could have gone on horseback or possibly sailed by sea to discover what was out there. <By the way Meatspace/Touchspace is the environment which physical matter and atoms and creatures such as you or I inhabit. I prefer the term Touchspace to Meatspace. However Franck tends to use the word Meatspace in his section of the book.> The top cone in the next diagram indicates the potential volume of Space-Time that they could have experienced. They could have encountered, visited and met other people, ideas and foods which existed in that cone. I've also included on the diagram another young person called Running Wolf. You noticed, I guess immediately, that Running Wolf and Jed the Inquisitive will never meet. Nor will they influence each other, share cooking tips or anything else. (Alternatively, if you prefer a more sober explanation, you could quickly go back in your mind 100 years and think about the average global speed with which ideas and learning could travel.)

100 years ago:

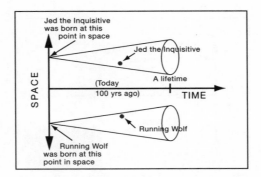

There is one major change to this scenario I have painted. Now, we can not only move through Meatspace/Touchspace at hundreds of miles an hour, (thousands in a space shuttle) but also the ideas, information and learning, from Running Wolf to Jed and back, all move at the speed of light, which is very fast indeed. In fact one of the funniest anomalies of the process of information transfer happens in organizations. Information traveling *between* organizations often moves at the speed of light to a fax machine or e-mail only to be printed out, sent to a mail room, stored for hours, moved about on foot, left in in-trays, carried home and back to work by car and then finally received and dealt with. In my experience inside organizations few things happen at the speed of light.

You see, once upon a time, two people would meet in a room or on a path and have a conversation. We would state where they met and had their conversation. It was obvious. It was in the room or it was on the path. However, now if you phone someone up, exactly where is the conversation taking place? Is it at your end? Or at their end? Or both ends?

<Reader to stay slightly puzzled at this point for at least 30 seconds>

Or perhaps, something which is both ends and also in-between but it isn't really a place? This room, this space, where your conversation takes place, is Cyberspace. So now with Jed and Running we could envisage them interacting in two environments, *Meatspace/ Touchspace* (see earlier note) and *Virtualspace/Cyberspace.*
Today:

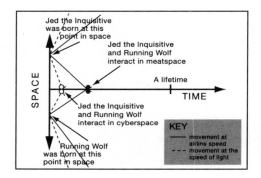

Of course the interaction in cyberspace is not only sooner, there may even be the possibility of a higher level of influence. Add to this, of course, the fact that in cyberspace the interaction need not only be limited to Jed and Running (in Meatspace/Touchspace the more people involved, the bigger the hall we need to hold them), but in addition anyone and, in theory, everyone on the globe could be involved. An added opportunity for cyberspace is that it is quite comfortable as the 'home' for information which has been transferred into digital representations. Have you ever wondered what happens when you send someone a fax?

<0.1 seconds of thought from you, since I am about to explain it next. And anyway it's very nerdish to understand such things>

Roughly, (not entirely true but true enough to suit my purpose) what happens, is that as the paper goes through the machine, the machine chops the page up line by line. In each line it chops the line into lots of very small rectangles. Then the eye of the fax machine looks at each square, one square at a time and asks, 'is this square black or white?' If it's black it writes a '1' and if it is white it writes a zero. Once a string of numbers has started to be generated it screams down the line to the other machine. One millisecond microscream per number one. The other machine listens to the screams assuming each scream to be a one and so on. It turns the screams into numbers, looks at the digits which it is receiving and if it sees a zero does nothing and if it sees a one, puts a black splodge into a cell on the paper on the other end. So we go from a piece of paper in Meatspace/Touchspace with handwriting (continuous analogue) through a process of digitizing (to create digital information), the digital information is then happy to move through cyberspace (or be stored in it, in the memory of the receiving fax machine, if the paper has run out) and finally back in analogue form into Meatspace/Touchspace.

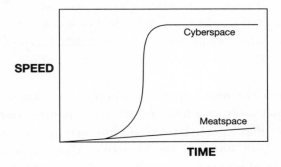

So far, most of us Meatspace/Touchspace creatures prefer to have our information available in Meatspace/Touchspace. We even claim not to be able to read things off a computer screen. We like to print things out so that we can touch and feel them. As cyberspace grows it makes less and less sense to bring anything into Meatspace/Touchspace at all. It makes far more sense to instead peer through the peephole into cyberspace, or to listen to the sounds it broadcasts than to keep moving information in and out of it. Cyberspace manages information much better than Meatspace/Touchspace. And in cyberspace the concepts of volume and density don't really exist. Why handwrite a letter, type it up, print it out, fax it for an immediate response whilst posting another copy for legal coverage, receive it the other end on fax paper in the fax room, collect it from the fax machine, walk down the corridor to the room of the person who needs to see it and then to place it in a pile of other Meatspace/Touchspace artifacts and paper, read it and then purchase a large gray metal box with drawers into which the piece of paper is stuffed again alongside several thousand others? And then reply, by reversing the entire process, when you could have typed it straight into a digital format and sent it directly to the person you want to receive it? And add nothing in volume or mass to what they need to store the message? Bizarre! Generations to come will not believe that we did such convoluted things. Looking back with humor, they will conclude that we were at a very stupid stage of human evolution.

If cyberspace exists, it exists in our minds. Just as both people in the phone conversation thought the conversation existed. Because it exists in our minds, it exists as we perceive it and only as we perceive it. It exists only so far as it interacts with us in Meatspace/Touchspace. Cyberspace is a world which has the effect of being real but actually only exists to us when we perceive it in our minds. It is a *virtual* world. The vast size of this virtual space world is terrifying.

<Reader to take a little time here to consider how long it would take them to read everything on their own computer – their company's network – the internet>

And it is inhabited by creatures we will never directly meet, agents, viruses, background programs and the like.

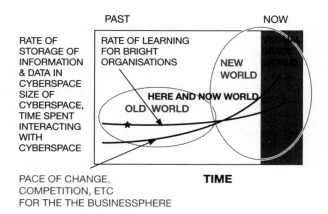

The **Old/New World** schism is primarily defined by *changes in reality and learning* whilst the Next Worlds, **Here and Now** World/**Virtual Space** disjunction is defined by *interactions and movement*. You see, an organization can be in the New World, operating as a New World organization without being in Space World.

For the rest of this book I shall cover all aspects of the New World. The rules apply whether you are in the subset of New World which is in the Here and Now, or if you have begun to use interactions and activities primarily in Space World. If you wish to know more about Space World specifically I guess you could always e-mail me.

So what? I love driving and I love flying. Two different machines in two different environments. When you drive, it tends to be a one, and at most, two dimensional experience. You can see the road and road surface on which you are travelling. In general, the controls do not tend to interact. That is, accelerating doesn't swing you round to the left. When you fly a helicopter it tends to be a three dimensional experience. You can't see the medium through which you travel and the controls certainly do interact. Two realities. Driving you tend not to move your head from side to side. Flying you do so, rhythmically, high, ahead and low, as you scan the horizon. Everything is affected by the different environments: the streamlining of the machines, their components, even how you speak.

Well, for a start, the two worlds, Old and New bring different realities. The realities give rise to different assumptions about how it all works, which in turn determine the actions people take, and finally it determines our mind-sets and how we interpret any additional incoming data.

Old World realities	New World realities
Possible to learn faster than the world changes.	World changes much faster than your ability to learn.
Constraints in cyberspace.[5]	Constraints in Meatspace/ Touchspace.[6]
Change is usually an event. Linear and first order.	Change is often non linear and not first order.
Change is often perceived as a 'step change' and a clear discontinuity.	Change is often alterations and may show emergent effects.
Ways of working are valid until it is obvious that they are invalid.	Everything should have a 'sell-by date'.
Local is defined by movement of atoms.	Local is defined by interactions and movement of information.
Human beings exchange goods and services in order to survive themselves.	Human beings exchange goods and services in order to survive themselves.

Think about the example below. The sequence leads to re-inforcing an Old World behavior. That of supervision and classical management.

OLD WORLD REALITY: Constraints in cyberspace.

↓

It is only possible to know what someone else is doing by being there or being close to them

↓

If I have many people doing many things, I need some people to be there to check up on my behalf and to keep tabs on what is going on but I also need them to be here with me to tell me what is happening. They must report back

↓

I need a supervisory grade

↓

Supervision is the only way to make sure that people are doing what they should

↓

The larger my organization the more levels of management I need

↓

Things are not working out quite as planned. Forecasts aren't met

↓

Since the only way to control is to be there I need even more on-the-job supervision

In a New World environment as information becomes more available in an appropriate format and as we begin to understand how to utilize the multi-interactions of virtual space world, *training replaces supervision* as the key route to getting the desired outcome. As the structure of the organization no longer needs to mirror the linear up-down information flows, it becomes more important to design for the virtual space world than for the Here and Now World. It doesn't take a genius to realise that the role of management is going to change beyond recognition. I believe that the term will remain as an anachronism, an ancient artifact, rather like talking about 'dialing' on a key-pad phone or the 'bonnet' or 'trunk' of a car. It will remain because it is too difficult to change, like decimalising time, switching to ten hours in the day, one hundred seconds per minute (or is that deci-hour?). I believe it will remain because I believe in the short term salary structures and grades will remain out of synchrony with the New World and as a result, even New World players will resort to Old World speak in order to get themselves well paid employment.

I know that it's taken me a long time to get round to explaining the point I made earlier about Learning Organizations. I suggested that becoming a Learning Organization (many organizations' holy grail) will not return us to the Old World, the world of certainty and linear extrapolation. I don't believe that becoming a Learning Organization will make 'everything wonderful' again. What do you think will happen as your organization becomes a Learning Organization? First, you will understand the environment. Then you will seek to exploit it. And in trying to get advantage from the environment you will generate more change. As most interactions across the globe are now interlinked, you will alert Jed and Running and all the people in between, who will react to what you're doing. And as *one change leads to another* all that will happen is that the world will change even faster, accelerating away from you and what you have learnt.

I like that last bit. It is almost as if you start off with an idea. A good idea, and yet as you implement it something goes wrong. A whole set of things emerge, which you hadn't foreseen. Somehow your journey ends up in the wrong place. Someone should write a book about that. Great idea! I'll consider doing that.

C — SURPRISE!!!

S/he's not dumb.
Surely s/he would have seen it coming.
Wouldn't s/he?

A word about emergence

It's been fashionable for some time to talk about chaos theory, its off-spring complexity theory, and the three more memorable phenomena of this school of thought, namely **emergence, self similarity** and **increasing returns**. Emergence is the more popular of the three. It has better examples associated with it. And in addition, it's much easier to make films and documentaries about. I'm sure you've seen them. A short section about a single bee. Busy as always, buzzing around, making honey and then, all of a sudden, a picture of a hive and then the emergent phenomenon. Someone or something disturbs the hive and VOILA! A swarm. The presenter uses the 'E' word. The presenter's soothing voice says something like 'the swarming behavior you are now observing emerges through the interactions of complexity'. It is impossible to extrapolate from the actions of a single bee to this **'swarming behaviour'**. The presenter pauses to let this heavy concept sink in. But is it really true? Is there really no link at all between a snowflake and an avalanche? Single snowflake: falls from sky; many snowflakes: form drifts or blanket of snow. Can you spot any emergent behavior yet? I don't think so. Not until you add in a steep-sided mountain; plus a disturbance of some sort; and then you have an avalanche of such emergent power it will easily bury you alive. It is the **combinations** we need to watch for. It is the *combinations from which patterns emerge*. It is these patterns against which you, as a New World manager, must be cautioned.

We expect birds to flock and bees to swarm, so most of us are not really surprised when it happens. But imagine if you had never seen flock of birds, the sheer and utter amazement you would experience from the phenomenon. It would be unexpected. Perhaps you would even call it a miracle. The combination of New World ideas with Real or Old World phenomena, I believe, can lead to emergent behavior you wouldn't otherwise predict. I believe that **emergence**, rather than being counter-logical, **is fully logical but not intuitive** until after the event. If you are lucky enough as I am to see life in snapshots, snapshots of many companies trying to cope with the Old World/New World dichotomy, some of these emergent patterns become less surprising. I hope you now realise that *both success and failure come from gradual development*. You may think that a particular strategy is succeeding whereas in fact it has failed. It failed perhaps when you used an Old World assumption last year. It has failed, only you don't know that yet. Time, God's way of preventing everything from happening all at once, means that it takes a while for the effects of the Old World decision to come to the fore. So you don't know yet and, thank goodness, nor does any one else, yet. This gives you time to create a remedy. Or perhaps there is an activity you think is failing, whilst in reality it is set to become your greatest triumph.

Of the other phenomena, I would like to wait until the start of a later section. Self similarity is discussed in the section titled 'Chunk it or Junk it!' whilst increasing returns is explored in the section titled, 'Loop it up'. Can you wait? Is that OK?

2

Cautionary Tales

Prologue

It's dark outside. Inside twelve people sit, one stands, in a rough circle. It's dim inside. Dim but bright enough to see the features of the faces of the individuals in the group. One person looks flushed, betraying their rushed and late arrival to the group. The light from three tall, thin, black uplighters bounces off the ceiling. A ceiling striped black and white as if a giant zebra were lying on its back above them. The black uneven beams adding to the dim but calming atmosphere. The black and white pattern of the ceiling is broken by the walls. White walls bordered or dissected by other black wooden beams. The black wooden beams which hold up the ceiling. A large fireplace on the north face of the room, which should be host to a real fire, is empty. It looks as if it would be wonderful lit. The red of the red bricks of the hearth betraying that it hasn't been host to any fires for a long time, if ever.

The person standing is saying, "Thank you all for coming. I hope that you will feel comfortable to share your stories. I believe that it is only by working like this, by working with a group of people from different roles in the organization and across different organizations, that we can all get a real insight into the patterns of the New World and perhaps some of its rules. Each of you has already told me your tale but I think that the real value of this evening will be for you to hear directly from each other." "Dialogue and discussion, not presentation and posturing," he states flatly, checking for affirmation which he re-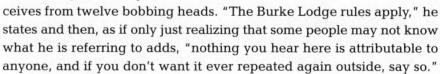ceives from twelve bobbing heads. "The Burke Lodge rules apply," he states and then, as if only just realizing that some people may not know what he is referring to adds, "nothing you hear here is attributable to anyone, and if you don't want it ever repeated again outside, say so."

He stands, feet slightly apart, in front of the large bay window. His black polo neck and black jacket in the zebra striped, black and white room make him look like a shadow of himself. A shadow with a small white rectangle cut out. Cut out just next to where a left lapel would be. A bright rectangle several inches across. Within the white rectangle, just below the grass-green, geometric symbol which is obviously some sort of logo, is the word 'Franck'. Franck looks steadily round the room, pausing at each face, waiting for a nod or a silently mouthed yes. "I will act as Moderator, asking questions and probing. But please feel free to ask questions yourselves. Try to make sure that these are questions for clarification and not for detail." He over-emphasizes the word clarification and the word detail. And then with energy says, "OK guys. Let's get on with it. Let's talk straight. Let's go to thoughts no one else has been to. Make it as interesting for each other as you made it for me. Let's see what we discover. After each of you recounts what you told me to the rest of the group I shall make some notes on the whiteboard." He points to a large electronic white-board in the corner behind an empty chair. "Please don't be distracted by what I write or draw, just keep the rhythm going." Then he raises the pitch and tempo of his voice slightly and says, "Onward into the New World!"

There is a short but earnest round of applause. He moves to sit down. As he does so he passes near one of the uplighters. The light from it reflects briefly off the top of his head. Now he, like all his com-panions, is sitting in a contraption which looks more like a giant black spider than a chair. It looks like a large piece of pipe-cleaner bent into the shape of the skeleton of a dead chair. There is a silence and then one of the group speaks.

<At this point, if you were watching a film or the TV, you would expect the screen to either become misty, or for wavy, out of focus, vertical lines to invade your picture. This symbolism in the visual arts media is used to represent the fact that you are going backwards in time. The piece of film you then watch is acted in the present tense although it actually occurred a long time before. This format is a favorite of soap opera directors, directors of cheap who dunnits and occasionally, great masterpieces. I have searched hard for an equivalent symbol for use with the written word and found none. Net result:- you have to pretend that these stories are each episodes in the past of the people at the current evening gathering meeting with the facilitator, Franck.>

The Firste
THE TALE OF THE EMPOWERING MANAGER

I'd done it – I should have known better. I'd almost managed to lose my job and 300 other peoples'. But could I have known better, or should I? The way I saw it, at the start, was quite straight forward, quite clear. Business is tough. Our customers each want something different. When you operate across the world you have to deal with the things which remain the same around the globe **and** the things that change from country to country and from customer to customer. It was absolutely essential that we should optimize our responses to customers locally. But we also had to standardize what we did right the way across the organization, after all, we didn't want a customer visiting two of our operations in different towns to experience completely different levels of service. The way I saw it, was that I really only had two choices. In order to *get it right both locally and right across the organization* we needed to align our overall business resources efficiently through a formal process and tackle issues as planned. This meant that we should *maintain very tight controls on what people said and did across the organization*. However, on the other hand, in order to make best use of our resources, we should actually allow the individuals dealing with the problem, to respond locally and immediately to any of the issues or problems as they arise. This meant that we should *empower our people, wherever they were in the organization*. The two conclusions seemed incompatible[7]. And everyone else seemed to be keen on empowerment, so I'd decided that that was the way to go.

I'd made that decision in another place and at another time. Now and here I look across the brown, fake leather seats, over the bar and towards the door. I'm sitting in a corner of The Saracen's Sword. The atmosphere is stale. Old tobacco and beer haunt the air. To the left of the bar an open fire burns fiercely. Too fiercely. There is no spare fuel, wood, coal, old newspapers alongside the fire. The fierce blue flames and lack of fuel supplies tell me that the fire too is a fake. A fake fire powered by gas but made to look like a real open log fire. I nurse my drink and wait. I am waiting for Franck. I don't have to wait long before the door bursts open and, with a smile as warm as the wind which sweeps in with him is cold, he charges towards my table.

"Hi there mate," he says cheerily in an accent with a slight twang, "What are you having?"

"I'll have another one of these," I say holding my cup up so that he can see the black coffee.

"Ordered anything to eat yet?" he asks.

"No," I reply, "But I've had a look at the menu."

"What will it be then?"

"Under the circumstances I guess I'd better go for something healthy. At least I have my health," I remark under my breath, choosing a light turkey salad. I'm actually dying for a burger with chips.

Franck takes a millisecond to make his mind up and then ends up going for the same thing as me. He steps over to the bar and in seconds the order is placed. He takes a seat next to me. "So tell me about what has brought you all this way."

"I think," I say hesitantly, "I mean, I seem to have gotten myself into a bit of trouble."

"Oh?" he says curiously.

"Well," I say, relieved at being listened to and at once launching into my story, "let me tell you what I did. I think I did everything right but somehow..." My voice trails off.

"Take your time," he says in a soothing voice. A voice which I know is also lying. I know he has to be away to another meeting after lunch. I have an hour. Only an hour. I decide to get on with recounting my story.

"Somehow I've managed to get our organization into a real mess."

"Start from the beginning," he instructs.

"It all began when we started getting customer letters. Letters of both complaint and praise about our products, services and our prices."

Franck nods sympathetically. He really seems to be concentrating on what I'm saying. It is as if he has never had to listen to a similar problem before.

"Well the problem was that the contents of the letters were completely random or at least they seemed so. Some said we were too slow, others that we were too expensive, others thanked us for providing such good products and excellent service. As a management team we didn't know what to do about it."

"So what did you do about them?"

"Well, we would have ignored the letters but we'd fallen behind slightly on our revenue targets and quite significantly on our net profit targets. So, we felt that there was a need to increase the amount of selling on, and also to retain customers who had shown interest in us." Franck nods his balding head rhythmically. "Sounds like a good, sound strategy to me," he remarks supportively.

"We decided to look at ways of making the front-line staff more responsive and flexible. We thought, 'Sure, if the customers want a lower price they can have it but we'll cut back on the speed of service and the related costs and keep up the margins. And sure, if they wanted a faster response they could have it but we would flex the prices upwards to match.'"

Franck is listening intently, his eyebrows furrowed above hawk-like eyes.

"Just as we were coming to that conclusion we realised that we also had a problem with the development of new products and services. We had received a 'pipeline' report from head office in Seattle informing us of the number of new products and services in the corporate development pipeline. There was a real problem. The bulk of the products were designed for their local market and wouldn't sell in ours without significant adaptation." I moan, "Bloody typical of head office, always parochial, always just looking at everything from their own point of view. So we realised that we needed both new ideas for products and new ideas on how to adapt the pipeline products to our local markets."

"So you needed to adapt the pipeline products to your local markets."

"Yes," I say, encouraged by his intervention, "and that was when the third problem hit us. If we were to carry out any further development or project activity we needed more managers. Well, actually, after discussion we concluded that we needed more *leaders*[8]. But how were we to get more leaders? Our head count budget was frozen. And anyway the last time we had attempted to recruit anyone to help lead internal change we had drawn a blank. It was almost as if there was no one out there. Almost as if there was a global shortage of leaders."

"Let me just check that I've understood your problems. You need to be capable of responding to each customer in a personalized and tailored way."

I nod.

"At the same time you need to develop new product and service offerings and you have neither the ideas nor the people to lead the implementation of any ideas you do get?" The pitch of his voice rises to confirm that this is a question.

I nod firmly. "You've got it," I say, pleased he is following my argument. "So you see the three problems came together at just about the same time and with a flash of inspiration we solved all three simultaneously."

Franck interrupts, "By 'we' I guess you mean 'I'?"

I refuse to take all the credit. "It was a sort of group thing," I declare, playing it down. "'We' means the top fifteen senior managers and a couple of our young management cadre. We had an Away-Day to discuss what to do. After a lot of discussion we decided that the way to get round all three problems was empowerment."

Franck looks blank. I guess the solution isn't as obvious a solution as I'd thought.

"Don't you see?" I say imploringly, "Empowerment. Empowered front-line staff can handle each customer on their merits without having to refer back up a long chain of command for any change to the SOP."

"SOP?"

"Standard operating procedure," I respond for clarification. "Empowered staff can be asked and encouraged to modify the existing product and service offerings providing all the new ideas we need for the gap in the pipeline. And empowered staff have the accountability for delivering the implementation of the new ideas."

Franck is nodding. "Very neat," he says. "A very neat solution indeed," he almost applauds. "Sounds to me like you discovered a perfect solution to your problems." He lets his last statement hang in the air as if waiting for me to make sense of it for him.

I say, "I was delighted too. We were about to embark on a trendy modern management solution but not just as a fad but instead as a real solution to real problems we had identified."

Franck has a quizzical expression on his face. It is as if he wishes to ask me something really obvious but is far too polite to do so. For once my intuition works. I guess what's going on. "I know what you're thinking," I say. "You're wondering why I wanted to speak to you?"

"Mm yes," he replies cautiously.

"In theory it should all have worked out fine but the current situation is that we've lost a dozen of our best staff and we are about to be sued for four million. All this on top of the worst profitability figures we've seen for years."

"What happened?" he asks, "What went wrong?"

"You tell me," I say. "It all started just right. We launched an Empowerment initiative. We didn't want to over raise expectations so we started with the cover page of our in-house mag. We got no response from that so we organized a manager's briefing. Normal affair, nothing complex. I remembered your advice about people's reactions to change and the third Law of Change[9] and I was really careful to present the problem and give an opportunity for the managers to invent the solutions."

Franck nods approvingly, looking impressed at my skill as a change leader.

"I guess the biggest surprise at the briefing was the attitude of the managers. Most of them were very negative about the idea. I couldn't work this out. As the briefing progressed it turned into a full blown complaints session about the poor quality of training and development provided by the organization. There was also another vein on the lack of recognition of the loyalty people had shown towards the organization. And that the loyal ones were always left to fix problems that the organization had created for itself. It was bizarre. Here we were offering a suggestion which would solve some major problems and safeguard all our futures and instead all we were getting was resistance. We decided that if we were not getting interest and enthusiasm at that level, we should take the message right down the organization ourselves. By 'ourselves' I mean the gang of 15 who had hatched the idea."

"I can see how you would have come to that conclusion," he interjects. "So did you?"

"Yes we did," I state. "We tried. But the response at that level was even more baffling. Here were we offering them a chance for self determination, to be able to influence their own futures and there was a high level of disinterest. And all the questions were of the W.I.I.F.M. variety."

"Wiifm?" he repeats pronouncing the acronym as I just had, as if it were one word.

"What's In It For Me," I reply. "Well I'd have thought it was obvious what was in it for them, greater influence over their work etc. But they all only really seemed to be interested in getting more money." Lunch arrives on a round wooden tray.

"Coffee, orange juice, turkey salad, turkey salad," utters the waiter solemnly like a teacher in a roll call.

Franck looks up and says, "Thanks Roger," reading the young man's name off his name badge. "I say Roger, can we have another coffee, black, just the poison, but in a mug rather than in a cup. In about fifteen minutes."

Roger looks aghast. His initial reaction of terror, to hearing his name spoken out loud, has been followed by a look of confusion and perplexity about Franck's request. He replies, "I'm not sure that we are allowed to give you mugs. All the mugs are in the restaurant bar section."

Franck is being unhelpful, he is simply staring at Roger. Roger is now stammering over his words. "The coffee comes from the machine. It gets poured once I put in the order," he explains. "If I wait fifteen minutes it will be cold."

Franck is now grinning mysteriously. "Don't worry about it Roger," he says. "Just bring it as it comes, when it comes." Roger leaves with our money.

"What was that about?" I ask.

Franck waves his right hand dismissively and says, "Never mind. Let's get back to your problem with empowerment."

"Well I think we went over the top. We knew that *providing monetary incentives was the wrong way to go* because all that would happen would be that we would simply give away any extra money made. And we were putting ourselves at a disadvantage for the future. Would we have to pay for all future changes and improvements? So instead we went into a sales pitch, even inviting outside speakers to come and talk to staff about the joys and benefits of being empowered. The speakers were very good, they drove home the message of empowerment and the need to improve things."

"And?"

"It seemed to work. Over about a month we had adapted one of the new products to our market place and it was selling like hot cakes. Also our customer satisfaction index rose from 76% to 82%."

"Sounds like success to me."

"Yes it seemed so. Some customers even went so far as to suggest other additional products and services we could provide to them. They really seemed to be building a good relationship with us. It wasn't until much later that we discovered that the new suggested offerings weren't very good for business profitability."

Franck is nodding and then he asks, "Did any other changes happen which did not help improvement to the bottom line?"

"Mmm," I say, thinking briefly, 'not really'.

Franck seems slightly surprised. "Did your staff do anything to 'improve' things, like changing the furniture or printing brochures or...?"

"Thinking about it again, yes they did. Yes, it's true. As the whole thing started to roll we kept getting ideas from the staff. Some we weren't so keen on but we didn't know how to turn them down without turning them off. So we went with them. We let them through as long as they were improvements."

"Improvements[10], eh?"

"Yes," I reply, unaware that I have just walked into a trap.

"And how did you know if something was an improvement?"

"Well," I remark, "it made things better."

"Better eh?" comments Franck raising a right eyebrow and tilting his head quizzically to the left.

"Yes. Better," I say.

"Carry on," he says, so I do.

"I was pleased with progress. So pleased in fact that I e-mailed Corporate in Seattle explaining the progress we had made with our localised services. And then it turned pear shaped."

Franck silently tilts his head to the right whilst raising his eyebrows. The impression is a definite "Keep talking". He is munching away hungrily.

"I'd been hearing good reports about how the staff were feeling and how positively customers were responding to our new approach and then one evening I took home the sales reports to study them in detail. In general there was a lag of about a month between receiving volume sales information and receiving the financials. Looking at the sales report I noticed that the volume of sales was up significantly but so were the costs and at the same time the revenues were down. But the costs were all in really unusual categories. It was as if our staff were bending over backwards to give the customers what they wanted, often by spending from other budgets. They also seemed to be delighting the customer using the most basic technique of simply giving the money away by dropping prices at the least hint of customer pressure."

"What did you do?"

"Nothing at first. I thought it best to talk to the others to see what they thought. I arranged a meeting for the day after. It was then that the first bomb shell struck."

"Bomb shell?"

"I discovered that one of our empowered staff had committed us to a $300,000 purchase without securing the customer order first. And that the customer had decided not to buy from us."

"Oops!" says Franck.

I react. "No, not Oops!" I exclaim. "Catastrophe!"

"It's the most bizarre thing ever. *You tell people that they are empowered and they interpret that as, 'I can do what I want without telling anyone else'*". I shake my head in despair. If they had asked Credit Control they would have discovered that the customer had been on the 'at risk' register for a fortnight. It was unlikely that they would or could actually buy anything costing that much".

"So you want to talk to me about how to fix the problem."

"No, I think I can fix it. What I want to know is how I could have avoided getting myself into this mess. You see the reasons we went for empowerment are still there, so we either need to make it work or we're back where we started. No, we are back," I struggle for the right words, "worse than where we started".

Franck looks thoughtful for a moment. Then for a moment too long. I realise that he is trying to finish off his mouthful, and then he says, "You said *first* bomb shell."

"Yes," I reply, guessing what's coming next.

"That implies more than one," he says insightfully, but without having to use any intellectual power.

"The second is a bit embarrassing. We fired him immediately but he is threatening an unfair dismissal claim."

"What happened?"

"Well in a nutshell, one of our managers managed to reduce the costs of one of our raw materials by ten percent."

"And you fired him?" questions Franck in disbelief.

"Only because he handed the contract to one of his friends and as a result, we discovered, got himself a free holiday in Spain."

"I can see why he is threatening unfair dismissal"

I hang my head despondently. "It all looked so promising. It was exactly what all the theory says. We freed people, gave them the opportunity to achieve their potential and look what's happened. I think I've lost all my faith in human nature," I say in a flat monotone.

I notice that Franck is glancing at his watch pretending hard not to. I look pointedly at mine. We have about half an hour left. He gestures towards my untouched salad. "I'm glad I ordered something cold, a hot meal would have been inedible by now. Can I try summarizing just to make sure that I've understood what you're saying? It sounds to me as if you carried out a set of actions to empower your staff but as a result a whole new set of problems and issues have emerged which you hadn't anticipated."

I nod. It's my turn to stay silent and munch. "Do you know why this sort of thing happens?"

I shake my head. This salad tastes a lot better than it looks. It must be the dressing.

"Do you remember saying how bizarre it was that when you started talking to the managers you had expected support for the idea and instead you got resistance?"

"Yes," I mumble.

"You were carrying out a single action and you expected that single action to cause just one effect, that of getting support from your managers."

I nod again.

"Instead it caused many effects, one of which was to heighten their level of insecurity. Your actions made them worried. Worried that you intended to replace them and their jobs with your other staff and that if it all went wrong you would be hands off and leave them with the problem to fix."

I nod again, but slower this time, now realizing what had led to the bizarre behaviour.

"And later you told me of the high levels of enthusiasm which some customers had towards what you were doing and how they had begun to suggest other service offerings you could provide, although unfortunately the costs of these were high by comparison to the returns."

I nod again, jerkily this time, not quite knowing where this part of the conversation is leading.

"It seems to me," he states, "that you have experienced emergence." He makes it sound like an encounter with extraterrestrials.

"Emergence?" I repeat with an inflection to highlight my lack of comprehension.

"People are only confused by emergence because they assume 1:1 linear causality in all actions and don't realise that other causes mix in with their plans and create often unobvious, complex but predictable results."

"Huh?" I grunt with my mouth full.

"Don't worry about the general case, let's just deal with your specific problem in the time we have available. May I ask you a very personal question?" he says curiously.

I'm unsure about the change in the tone of the discussion but, like most people, I like to act as if I have nothing to hide so I say, "Yeah sure."

"When," he asks, "was the last time someone actually said to you that they thought you could or could not be left to make your own decisions?"

I think momentarily. I can't think of any point where that has happened at work. "Can't think of any time at work," I reply.

"Not just at work and perhaps not even in recent years?"

I pause. "In that case I can't think of anything remotely like it, at least not since I was a teenager."

"Precisely!" he replies delighted. "That's it. That is exactly it. As a teenager, the fights and struggles were because you had spent all your life **dependent** on others. Dependent on your parents and now you wanted to demonstrate that you were independent."

I nod. I can't see where this is going.

"Your organization hires people and then for the next 40 years of their lives controls them, telling them what they can and can't do. Sets the time for bedtime and such like. Makes them get permission even to spend £20. Convincing them that someone somewhere up the organization knows all the answers is part of the process. And then, all of a sudden, out of the blue your 'parents' announce that you have to fend for yourself. How would you feel?"

"Terrified," I reply, still not sure what this has to do with my problem.

"Would you definitely embrace the announcement with open arms?"

I begin to see his point. Not completely surprising that we did not receive overwhelming support for offering empowerment.

Franck is still talking. "I think that when your colleagues at work finally heard what you were saying, they heard it as something new, uncharted territory and so reached back to see if they had ever had a similar experience of breaking free. And there it was, teenage rebellion. The move from having to do as your parents said, to completely ignoring them and doing your own thing."

Franck is being obscure again. I say, "So?"

"You said that a simple phone call to the credit controllers would have avoided one of your problems."

"I don't get it," I say flatly.

"You say 'empowerment', so they hear **'empowerment'**, they hear it and **interpret** it as a move away from **dependency** to being **independent**. Whereas what you were after was a shift from **dependence** to **interdependence**. *Interdependence: a recognition that our organization is a linked system and that we really only succeed if others succeed*[11]. Instead they act like teenagers and instead of working together they simply try to do it all on their own."

"Shoot!" I whistle softly as the realization dawns.

"Now add that to the fact that you forgot to tell them what they were empowered to do. That the name of *the game was to make money, **not** to generate ideas or customer satisfaction*. You forgot to mention that customer satisfaction was a means to the end of making money. A great means but not the end itself. You forgot to tell them how to check if an idea was any good by checking whether it made money or not. Remember a *change is an alteration* whilst an *improvement* is an action *which takes you closer to your goals. Change and improvement are not the same thing*[12]. Without telling them what the goals were, they never stood a chance."

I think I have my mouth open. My brain is concentrating on what I'm hearing and has forgotten to send 'close' signals to my jaw muscles.

Franck notices the effect he is having on me and checks I'm still with him. I nod slack jawed to indicate that I am. "For empowerment to work your people need to have personal accountability. Remember how taken aback Roger was by me using his name. I don't think he saw himself as empowered."

"I wondered why you were using his name. Was all that discussion with him just to prove your point?"

"Yes. But it was more than one point. Not only did I use his name to discover how much accountability he felt comfortable with, but also I wanted to check his capability."

"Capability?"

"Can they do what they are being asked to do? Do they have the *skills* and *capability*? It must also be clear that any *risk* they enter into on behalf *of* the *organization* is as much of a *risk to them*[13]. And finally can they be *trusted* not to operate in a criminal way?"

I listen, knowing that what Franck is saying all adds up. I listen knowing that he has explained the causes of my current crisis. Like always, I wish we'd spoken sooner. "I don't know what to say," I say apologetically. "The way you dissect my problems it makes it all seem so obvious. That was really useful, how can I repay you?"

"You could come to a New World exploration meeting I'm planning next month."

"Done," I agree.

Now he is looking directly at his watch. No more sneaky sideways glances. "I'm afraid," he says, "that I have to be somewhere else". With that he rises, in one smooth movement turns, pull his jacket on and motions, with his head, towards the door. I rise and leave the table just behind him. We burst through the fake wood doors into the real sunshine outside. I think it's turning out beautifully again.

<Wavy lines again and back into the present.>

Franck rises from his seat, walks up to the electronic copyboard in the corner of the room and writes:

- *linking – loops*
- *other people – not alone*
- *And!*
- *purpose – change vs improvement Money making.*

And then he sits down again. There is a murmur as the people present try to make sense of his notes. He gives them no time to reflect and simply barks, "Next?" an order disguised as a question.

The Seconde
THE UNCERTAIN STRATEGIST'S TALE

Two billion pound turnover and one of the fastest growing businesses in Europe and I'd blown it. How could any one fail with built-in advantages like that? I had. I feel such an idiot.

I'm sitting in the departure lounge at Heathrow opposite a balding man. And for some reason, pouring out my heart to him. I don't usually tell almost complete strangers all about the things I've done wrong but Franck seems so genuinely interested and supportive that he has fooled me into dropping my guard. My attention strays and I turn slightly to my left looking out of a wall-sized window at a white and red 737 taxiing gracefully past us.

"And so what happened next?" he asks.

I have just told him the background to my sorry state. I've explained how, in spite of our explosive growth in volume, our margins started to shrink and I was given the job of 'thinking about what to do about it all'. "Well," I say immediately, "it seemed that the market was less and less interested in paying for the services we'd been supplying. When we started, the main competition was one large organization. In the past we had studied their weaknesses and focused on how to satisfy the customer in those specific areas. As a result, Bingo! We now had a £2bn organization. The competition, who had been a sleeping, lumbering giant, seemed to have got their act together, so that service levels which two years previously were legendary, were now commonplace. If we were to *make any money now and in the future* we would have to *concentrate on doing even better what we already did well today*. This would mean that we would have to *concentrate all our best people and key resources on improving the service offering we currently provide*[14]."

On the face of it, this was an obvious option. We already had in place all the performance and appraisal infrastructure which had kept us growing so effectively. What we really needed to do was to get the message out that we needed to be ahead again and to encourage people to look again for chinks in the armor of our traditional competition.

There was one wrinkle though. Perhaps more like a big crease. Some of our business was not only being lost to our traditional competitors but also to new emergent competitors. The difference with the new competitors was that they weren't playing fair. They weren't competing head to head. For example, whilst we were offering customers purely service, their service was backed up with comprehensive guarantees. But the worst part was that because they were using the new technologies to provide the new services, they had a completely different cost base to us and whereas we made money directly from the customer they also made money by distributing hardware on behalf of OEMs. This was what frightened us. It meant that they could continue competing the margins down way below the level at which we would cease to be profitable and by creating a commodity business could drive us out of business. This meant *that in order to make money both now and in the future* we would have to *find ways of doing things significantly differently*. In order to achieve this we would have to *focus the efforts of all our best people and resources on creating solutions for the future*[15]."

I finally pause, waiting for a reaction. Franck says, "What a dilemma. Stay with your core traditional business and risk the chance of losing to an emergent industry or concentrate on creating a new industry and risk losing out to your traditional competitors. What a bummer!"

He has summarized the problem very well. "You've summarized that very well," I say in a congratulatory tone. Suddenly the airport tannoy cuts in announcing a flight. I pause to wait for the announcement to end. It's not my flight and judging from the look of disinterest on Franck's face it's not his either.

"Carry on," he urges.

"It was mid financial year so we didn't have any formal way of getting people's attention, so we held a large management briefing to inform managers about the need to challenge themselves in order to regain the margins we'd lost. I think we talked about the importance of innovation in delivering business results."

"How was it received?"

"Surprisingly well. But here's the sting in the tail. When we looked at the figures a month later, rather than improve they'd actually gotten worse."

"Why was that?"

"I did some grapevining and discovered that almost every manager had interpreted the message only partly correctly. They knew that something had to be done and what they had done was try to sell more or produce more. They had looked at their annualized targets and simply pulled them forward. They had sold more volume but the customer pressures on margins meant that the overall profitability was worse. Almost no one had tried to sell anything different to the customers."

Franck has a quizzical expression on his face.

"I guess what was happening was that they were trying to meet our demands whilst satisfying the annual targets we'd set them."

No change to the expression.

I explain, "Their targets determined their appraisal results, bonuses, promotions and so on. They would have been mad to abandon them simply to satisfy our immediate demands."

The expression has changed to one of comprehension. I continue. "I was responsible for delivering strategy and so I suggested that we had time out. We held an Exec. Retreat to discuss what we were going to do about getting people to do things differently. It was a typical two day event and we hired a facilitator to help us. I guess I was lucky. I chose someone I'd never worked with but she had a good reputation so I'd taken the risk. The first day covered most of the standard stuff SWOTs, PESTs and so on and then on the second day the facilitator started urging us to be creative with our solutions. She talked us through some truly remarkable case studies. Companies who had re-invented their industries. Others who had grown from minnows to dominate the globe. I think she also flattered us by constantly referring to our own phenomenal growth and placing us firmly in the league of these super-companies."

I pause, checking that Franck is still following what I'm saying. I also glance at my watch to see how much time I have left before my flight. It was a good idea of Franck's to meet here at the airport whilst we were both waiting for flights. It was good use of the time. Usually I browse the shops or camp out in the lounge pretending to make important phone calls.

"What happened next?" he asks.

"We got pretty fired up. We talked big. We talked about reinventing the industry. For some reason I still don't understand to this day, the idea of reinventing the industry captured all our imaginations. From the MD all the way down. Instead of our usual politically correct responses, my colleagues and, I must admit, I started to get excited about it. I can't remember us showing emotion towards any action or initiative for years. It must have been the effect of the facilitator, I guess," I add thoughtfully. "Anyway, it all made sense. We would go against the new competitors with energy. We would focus on customer product needs and deliver the need at the point of highest value. This would grow our margins and at the same time it would protect our future income, putting severe pressure on both traditional and new competitors. We even coined a term for it. We talked about moving from CATS (Carrying-out Also-ran Technical Services) to DOGS (Devilishly Opportunistic Good Stuff)." I pause waiting for a response.

"Cats and dogs?"

"Well we started by calling them pots and pans (pretty amazing new stuff) but we couldn't find an acronym for pots."

Franck nods, baffled.

I decide to continue my story quickly. "Anyway, the upshot of it was that we decided to concentrate on doing new things in a new way to reinvent the industry. We felt that there was so much history and performance measurement encouraging people to do more of the same, to do slightly better what we already do today. We felt that we should get our people aligned onto the future."

"Given the background, that seems to make sense," he comments. "So what's the problem?"

"Well it didn't work too smoothly," I say. "We needed to get everyone working toward the new goals so that we could meet and *overcome the strategic*[16] *problems* we needed to move from reactive tactics to develop a longer lasting philosophy. To achieve this we needed *to create and actively communicate a clear vision.*"

I can tell from his expression that he can't see the problem.

"Don't you see? The problem was that the strategic problems were immediate. So we needed to frequently re-focus on strategic pressures. That suggested almost the antithesis of what we felt we needed to do. It meant that rather than look too far to the future we should instead be *creating and monitoring short term challenges*. This was the point at which all the camaraderie and team spirit we had built up during our retreat evaporated. Two thirds of the exec wanted us to press forward with the ideas and vision we had developed and concentrate our efforts on making sure that all our people were focused on creating our new offers. And then there was the other third. They were moaning and dragging their feet complaining about their existing work load. Just like dinosaurs complaining that they were far too busy becoming extinct to evolve. Fortunately the majority included our MD. So forward to the new industry it was."

"So your MD stifled the debate and insisted on one of the ways forward?" he asks in a flat tone which I interpret as disapproval.

"Not so much stifled," I reply, "more like showed decisive action for once. It was just as well because the next stages also went just like a dream. We knew we had to get the vision across and we had to enthuse people to actually do something different in their day jobs in order to bring the whole thing to life. We did all the right things. We canvassed the key opinion leaders. We developed a one day event to communicate the messages. We got the directors to run the event, rather than using an external speaker, that way we demonstrated commitment. We made it interactive and finally we made absolutely sure that every one literally went through the process. The way we achieved that was to hire a large warehouse and kit it out with a stage PA system and rows of tables each fitted with a microphone. That meant that the sessions of up to 250 people could be interactive and people could ask questions about anything they were unsure of. Can you imagine?" I say, my eyes shining with the excitement of remembering, "**two way dialogue**[17] not just **talking at them**. It was fabulous!"

Franck is nodding attentively as I reel off the list of things we did to get the initiative going, obviously drawn in by the enthusiasm in my voice. "You felt you needed to involve **everyone** fully?" he asks.

I'm barely thinking about his question as I reply, "Sure. We wanted to roll out the new strategy and do it fast."

"And?" he asks.

"That was it. We'd done it. There was enthusiasm for the initiative. Our people felt that they had permission to explore and create the new organization. We were absolutely delighted." I pause for effect again. "Can you imagine the feeling of power and success?" We had turned on 2000 people. We had run the workshops over a three week period. The workshops were followed by the directors 'walking the talk'. We spent a fortnight walking the corridors department to department, shaking hands, answering questions. It was rolling. We had reached critical mass. They were going for it. They were committed. And then..."

"And then?"

"And then we realised that almost four months had passed. We realised this and noticed the figures. Customer satisfaction was the worst ever. Our satisfaction index had collapsed. It seemed that we had become completely inwardly focused through our initiative. Our customers felt ignored. Sales were down too. But the real shock was the costs. Costs had gone astronomical."

I'm watching the expression on Franck's face as I tell him all this bad news. His brow is furrowed, his jaw muscles are rhythmically tensing and releasing.

"The costs had skyrocketed because we had started so many projects simultaneously. However, none of the projects were showing much progress because we were spending all our time in meetings and since there were too many projects the meetings led one to another without any time to do any actual work in between. My colleagues had been dragged into sponsoring so many projects that they were also out of the loop. It took a further week before we could get past unbreakable commitments and organize a meeting, to decide what to do about the impending crisis."

"Is that what you really want from me, to find out what to do about the crisis?"

"Yes and no," I say shaking my head from side to side as I reply. "I guess what I really want to know is how it all went so right and then all went so wrong. I mean, we'd achieved what hundreds of companies only dream about when they launch initiatives and yet we were failing as a business and failing fast."

"I see. First, before I comment, tell me what happened at the meeting."

"Well the outcome was simply to give it another couple of months to see what it yields. And that's it. It's probably the right thing, not to panic. But it feels scary. It started off a bit tense. About half an hour into the discussions one of my colleagues described it as selling off the present to pay for the future. It was a good description. We all laughed. It broke the tension. Usually companies are accused of being short-sighted and doing the opposite, compromising the future to survive today."

Franck smiles warmly.

"What I want to know is how could we have avoided being in this situation. We seem to have done everything right so how come...?" My voice trails off as I pass the baton to Franck.

Franck takes a deep, long breath. "In the Old World[18] environment efficiency was a clear route to success."

I nod.

"You improved your chances of success by doing few things but doing them **all** the same way. In a world where if you were smart enough you could learn faster than the world changed, it made sense to do things one way *or* another." For some reason he stresses the word 'or'.

"You will find," he states, "that the word 'or' is firmly etched into the Old World part of your brain." He pauses, focuses on my face and asks, "Why did you feel that you had to put **everyone** in the organization through your process?"

It's the same question he'd asked earlier. I reply quickly, "To get buy-in. You need buy-in for this sort of thing."

"So what you are saying, is that it was **absolutely crucial** that you had to get buy-in from everyone, **at the same time**?"

I pause briefly. I think silently to myself, 'No, not everyone.' I reply, "but eventually we would have to get everyone on board."

Franck raises his left eyebrow a centimeter. "Perhaps eventually. But why did you feel you had to work with everyone, all at once? Were there areas of the business where you might have made gains earlier? Maybe even given them slightly different messages? Maybe you were thinking that it was either the old way of operating **or** the new way." Again, for the second time in three minutes he over stresses the word 'or'.

'It's true,' I think, 'we were assuming that the most efficient route would be to give the message to everyone. We justified it by thinking that we were concerned about the propagation of mixed messages.'

"You're right," I say, "We were fooled by our need to appear efficient, we thought it made sense to be fair to everyone. Being fair meant treating everyone equally. Now I see that we would actually have been fair to treat every one differently. It was unfair to treat people equally. Unfair on the organization and unfair on the people. It didn't give them the best opportunity to succeed. It's almost as if..."

The airport announcement system cuts in again drowning my words. This time it announces my flight, delayed for half an hour and a second flight, Franck's, as a 'last call'. It's not fair. He rises up grinning down at me in mock triumph. For that brief moment in time I don't care anything about what we've said before or any conclusions I might have reached. I exclaim, "It's just not fair!"

<< Wavy lines wavy lines... back to the present.>>

As the account ends the listeners appear thoughtful. One listener looks particularly perplexed. "What about efficiency?" s/he demands. There is no reply. Franck is busy adding to his notes on the white board.

One of the other listeners says, "I guess it makes more sense to achieve the results effectively than to just be efficient?" The statement is phrased as a question inviting other comments.

"I guess it depends on which industry you're in," says another, responding to the invitation.

At the whiteboard, Franck clears his throat. "Sorry to be an ogre but, ground rules. Let's save the discussion until we've heard all the accounts."

On the white board behind him have been added two new bullet points:

- *fair = equal* ➡ *fair = different; unfair = equal*
- *or* ➡ *and*

The Thirde
THE TALE OF THE CUSTOMER-FOCUSED MANAGER

I t's so frustrating! What's the point in knowing all there is to know about your customer segments, if you don't actually get any benefit out of it? Two years of my life, my time, and now everyone pays lip service to it but no one actually uses the data. It can't be because everything is working well because it isn't. Our average prices have been squeezed down and along with them the margins. Yeah, sure, I know that for a while they took a bit of notice. For a while we actually tried to concentrate on customer needs. For a while it looked really promising, but now..." I pause, sighing, my head shaking from side to side like an ancient marionette, "Would you believe it, our customer satisfaction indices are falling again? It seems as if, as the satisfaction levels fall, we promise **more** to customers. But it's far easier to promise than to deliver so I suspect that all we are doing is making sure that we fail to meet expectations. We are making sure that **our** improvement is not happening at the same rate as **their** expectations are rising. I fear that all that will happen next is that the satisfaction will fall even further. And yet whenever I try to raise the issue, I just get stonewalled."

A semi-sympathetic voice asks, "Stonewalled? What do you mean stonewalled?"

We are sitting in a meeting room on the first floor of a hotel. This hotel, like all the others in the chain, is situated close to a motorway on the outskirts of a town. This room, like all the others in the series on this floor, has the standard issue flipchart, wall hung screen, rectangular wooden box complete with pens, tippex, blu-tack and six, gray, hard-backed swivel chairs. The room obviously began its life as a bedroom. The clues are everywhere, sockets and switches a third of the way up the wall, an en suite toilet (perhaps for high stress meetings?). A sign of the times, a sign of transforming to meet customer needs. Amazing how hotels have been transformed from places where travelers went to spend a night of sleep in comfort, into multi-functional virtual offices, meeting rooms for companies, where executives go to spend their days in workshops and off-site meetings.

I begin to answer. "I'm not really sure," I say, "In most of the discussions I have about why people aren't using the information we have available, it's almost as if," I hesitate as I try to find the right words, "it's almost as if we are talking at crossed-purposes. To me it seems obvious that *to continue to be profitable, we need to encourage customers to give us and to continue to give us, a decent amount of money for the things we offer them.* I think that the best way to achieve that is to *make sure that we are giving them something that they really value or need.* Often the people I am discussing it with, come at it from an entirely different angle. They seem to argue that it is obvious that in order *to continually generate profits, it is essential to beat the competition.*"

Franck is nodding. He must be thinking that the other angle also makes sense.

"But since the competition are far from dumb and almost as good as we are, the best thing to do is to *play to our strengths, utilize any factor or strategic advantages we possess and in fact concentrate primarily on making sure that we deliver what we are best at doing.* The customer doesn't really figure in this thinking. I mean, we are known in the industry for having available a few very good products."

Franck shrugs, "That also makes sense. I can see why you get stonewalled. You said it got better and now it was getting worse?"

"Yes, well," I glance sideways out of the window and across the eight lanes of multicolored movement, trying to think of how to explain things. I look back at Franck. "Let me give you the whole history. It will be much easier for you to understand. It all started a couple of years ago with our new General Manager. She decided that it was essential for us to be more customer-focused. Of course everyone agreed," I shrug my left shoulder, "it's only common sense. And then we tried to establish what that meant and whether we were already customer-focused. That was the first shock. We didn't actually have any information on our customers. We'd never bothered to collect any. That just demonstrated how little interest we'd had in customers in the past," I say, the incredulity still in my voice. Franck looks as if he's heard this problem before.

"Something had to be done fast, so we recruited a firm of market researchers and set them to work gathering customer information. They drew up a list of people to contact and interview including several of our own people. A month and a half later they presented the results."

"What did they discover?"

"You're going to laugh when I tell you the outcome."

"No, I promise I won't," he declares solemnly.

"They discovered that they needed to do some more work."

Franck stifles a guffaw which comes out instead as a rather rude snort.

"I told you you'd laugh."

He feigns remorsefulness. "I promise I won't laugh anymore. Please tell me what else happened."

"Well we gave them the time. And they produced several thick bound volumes of an immense report stuffed full of bar charts, pie charts, max-min charts and so on. The back-up data was very impressive. The problem was with the conclusions that they had drawn. They had placed our customers into four groupings."

"Why four groupings?"

"That was the question we asked too. All that work and they had served us up the good old MBA model of innovators, early adopters, etc. and they had done a similar thing for the product and service offerings we were providing, representing them all in a standard consultants two by two matrix, labeled as cows and dogs."

"Obviously don't know or understand about the New World," Franck remarks softly, almost under his breath.

"Pardon?" I say.

"I said that they obviously don't understand the New World. In New World markets, the product offerings and rates of change can be so rapid that many products are only taken-up over a short fixed period, only to be replaced by something entirely different which provides different benefits. I mean, is a notebook computer with an integral track ball, and internal adapter and all the portability and the lifestyle it offers, the same product as one which forces you to carry one of those ubiquitous black shoulder bags? Shoulder bags obviously designed by someone with the style and design skill of a lumberjack, so that all you can carry is a mouse and yards of black wire with a box stuck halfway along the length?"

I ponder for a second. Franck is right. The two things are actually different offers. If you look beyond the product you recognise that there is a whole set of intangibles. I also think of the fact that against my advice my mum has just purchased a desktop computer. Not because there isn't newer technology around, like notebooks, but because she wants furniture for her study. "You're right," I say finally, "I guess some people will continue to prefer the black bags for some time to come and may never wish to change. I guess in the New World, the concept of product life cycle is probably already dead." 'Look for example at the introduction of telecommunications into Eastern Europe, a life cycle model would not explain the simultaneous development of land based, digital and cable systems.' I nod sagely, understanding Franck's point.

Then to drive it home he says, "These days *time isn't always linear, sometimes it is parallel, folded in on itself*[19]."

But his last point doesn't drive it home. It simply serves to confuse. I thought I understood what he was saying but now I realise I don't. At least not fully. I decide to move back to ground I understand better. I completely ignore his last comment and declare, "The problem with the delay in receiving the research results and with the simple obviousness of the models they suggested, was that it gave the skeptics in the company time to organize and regroup. They argued that there was too much data. And anyway, the model was the same as they had learnt at business school a decade earlier and that they had been applying as a matter of course, without the extensive market research. But their real punch came from their argument that, if the segments were simply groups of people appearing at different points along a product life-cycle, then as long as you captured the innovators, the early adopters would follow and so on to the laggards. The logical conclusion was 'just beat the competition'."

"What was the response from your General Manager?"

"Controlled frustration would be the best way to describe it. She decided that the best way to get people to concentrate, was to set customer satisfaction levels for each area of business and to link the appraisal and performance of the senior managers to the customer satisfaction targets."

Franck smiles as he says, "Sounds like a good idea." The smile is lopsided and somehow I feel he is hiding something. "And then?"

"Well, we did even more research to establish the best way to measure customer satisfaction, to build a set of questionnaires and a method for gathering the information. We were quite surprised by the first round of customer satisfaction measures. They were much better than we had expected on the whole. There were some customers though, who were highly dissatisfied with us."

"Why do you think it came out that way?" he quizzes.

"I guess you can't please everybody," I remark glibly. "But anyway it was a start. It gave us a starting point. The various business heads then set about with working groups and task-forces within their business units to try to identify ways of improving the customer satisfaction. They must have done a good job because when the same parameters were measured six months later they had improved."

"All this sounds very good. I still don't see what you were so keen to discuss with me. What is going wrong?"

"Two things really. Over the past three months based on our standard questionnaire the average is roughly the same although falling. We have fewer and fewer 'very satisfieds' and 'not satisfieds'."

"This is based on your original questionnaire?" he checks for clarification.

"Yes of course," I reply. "Although, strangely we seem to be getting more letters of complaint."

"Why is that strange?"

"Well initially we simply interpreted it as an increase in customer expectations. That wouldn't have been too surprising, we've seen some new entrants to our market place recently and it wouldn't be surprising if they were affecting customers. But when we looked a bit closer at the letters, we realised that although that is a factor, they seem to be complaining about changes and improvements we think have made our offers better. They seem to think we have made them worse."

Franck raises his left eyebrow as if to quiz me further but instead asks, "And the second thing?"

"Our margins are getting worse and worse faster and faster."

He nods slowly as if figuring something out for himself. A brief pause and then remarks, "You know you said earlier that you were being stonewalled because there was an argument that your organization should concentrate its efforts on doing what it does best?"

"Yeah that's right," I reply remembering.

"And remember you told me that many of your colleagues were unimpressed by the segmentation results. Because they thought that if it represented lifetime segmentation then as long as you captured the innovators all else would follow as night follows day?"

"Uhuh."

"And you remember that one of your strengths is having a few very good products?"

"Mmuh," I say signalling agreement.

He slows his speech and lowers the pitch of his voice as he asks, "What do you think happens in any organization where people feel happiest delivering what they are best at and the organization has built a reputation around a few product offerings? How interested would they be in discovering different segments of customers with different needs?"

"I guess that they wouldn't be particularly interested in segmenting up their customers. And I guess it sounds like a lot more work on something they are not particularly interested in."

"Now," he says, leaning forward almost aggressively, "add to what you've just said, the fact that many of the people think that there is no real need for parallel segmentation. They are assuming that if each product or service offering follows a life cycle, there is no real need to provide different offers to different customers."

"I guess that explains the lip service I've heard," I remark, enlightened

"Now do you understand why your margins are still under pressure?"

"No, not really," I reply plaintively, embarrassed at my inability to see the link.

"If you are paying lip service to segmentation, it is unlikely that you have not rethought what to offer the different segments you are trying to serve. That means two things: firstly, you probably haven't realised that you can charge different amounts to different customers for the different offers which could mean higher margins on some. The second thing it means is that you probably haven't reconsidered redesigning the processes you use for providing appropriate offers to the customer groups. Without changing the actual processes it is difficult to provide offers that the groups actually want. So to satisfy the needs, you are forced to use only one dimension of freedom, Price. Few customers offer to pay **more** for the same offer, so to satisfy them you are pressured into reducing prices. This of course has a direct impact on your margins.

I'm stunned. It's so obvious. 'Of course, without segmenting effectively we can't design the best offer for each group. Without the design we don't know what our processes should actually look like. Without both of those we will find it difficult to actually change our business success.' I say, "What you are saying makes complete sense. That was really useful." Slowly I remember that he hasn't covered the first problem, the changes in customer satisfaction. I want to ask about this but I'm not sure how to do so without appearing to be unappreciative or greedy. Fortunately Franck rescues me.

"Help me," he says wistfully, "I'm not sure about the customer satisfaction falling, and those complaints you mentioned. I'll tell you my problem. I can't understand why the number of 'not satisfied' customers has decreased."

"I guess it's because we are providing a better service."

"I'd agree but for the fact that you seem to be getting letters from people who are not altogether happy." He frowns and then asks, "Can I ask you a very important question?"

"Of course."

"You know the targets and the bonuses your General Manager set?"

"Yes."

"Were the bonuses really substantial?"

"Yes, of course. She was keen to signal how important she felt that customer satisfaction was."

"Now tell me," he insists, "if you had a bonus dependent on a questionnaire sent to customers to measure how satisfied your customers were, and you were a smart manager keen to achieve this bonus, what would your options be?"

"Well," I reply, thinking only for an instant, "I could change what I offered them to make them more satisfied or eliminate the things we did which pissed them off."

"Anything else?"

I can't think of anything else. I shake my head slowly.

"Are you sure that there isn't one more angle?"

I'm still thinking. No result, and then it's obvious. "I could change my customers!"

"Precisely," he states triumphantly. "Too much pressure to improve the output from a sample could instead lead to people changing the composition of the sample. What do you think happens if your Business Unit managers change the composition of their customer base by actually getting rid of the most obnoxious ones?"

"Their satisfaction index will rise but also our revenues may decrease," I say with slow recognition.

"Worse!" exclaims Franck. Remember, *in the New World,* **time** is both **linear and parallel.** *Your most* **obnoxious customers are** *often* **invaluable** *in* **helping** *you to* **predict the linear aspects of time.**"
I must look baffled because he keeps explaining. "What I mean is, that they are probably giving you advanced warning of what members of other segments will be demanding in a month, six months time. You should love your most obnoxious, demanding customers, nurture them. Instead you encouraged your Business Unit heads to get rid of the only future echo you had."

I can see it's a problem but I don't see it's as much of a problem as Franck is making it out to be. "Maybe it's not such a big problem as you make it out to be," I challenge.

He smiles. He shows just too much of his teeth. I feel as if I have challenged him on the wrong topic. I feel that I'm about to receive a challenge right back. "Tell me," he insists, "In the New World environment, is a year a long time or a short time?[20] It's obvious a year these days is a tremendously long time. Anything can happen in a year."

"A long time," I reply. "Gone are the days when a one yearly review or budget actually served a useful operational purpose."

"Good." he says, "I'm glad we agree on that. If a year is a long time, then taking a week to respond to a customer need or request is actually quite a long time."

I nod in agreement.

"So do you think that being able to gain a month or two on your competitors would be a source of advantage."

Again I nod.

"And you're suggesting that having customers who tell you, a few months in advance, what you need to be doing next is overstated?"
I think, 'Oops'.

"In a business environment which is changing rapidly it is essential to understand that you also are part of that environment. You also are linked to it. Do you know," he asks with sincere interest, "what a first order system is?"

'A what!' I think in exclamation. I say politely, "No".

His eyes cast around as if he is searching frantically for something. "Mnnn," he groans as his brain seeks a solution. "Let me try this on you, a simple scenario. I'll make it a sad story just to get your interest. Simple situation – husband drinks too much. His wife is upset and worried about where all the over indulgence will lead and suggests to the man that he stops drinking. This makes the man upset. Feeling first that he is a failure and then feeling resentful towards his wife whom he feels has scolded him. He seeks solace. What do you think happens next?"

It's obvious. "He gets completely legless, I mean drunk, so that he can forget that he is failing," I reply.

"Precisely, because he is feeling resentful towards his wife there is no where to turn for solace except to the bottle. So he drinks more. Now what do you think happens?"

I say, "I guess his other half nags him to keep off the booze."

"Yes!" he exclaims in triumph, apparently delighted with the progress we are making. "The wife is now alarmed at the drunken state of her husband and tries even harder to get him to stop. She uses entreaties, begs, threatens. The intensity of her persistence growing as she realizes how important it is that he is returned to the straight and narrow as soon as possible." He pauses. I'm wondering where this is leading. He asks this time, "What happens next?"

"It's a vicious cycle. I guess the man ends up a complete liverless drunk and the wife talks herself into a stupor." I can see no link at all whatsoever between a drunk in a broken home and our obnoxious customers.

"How does it work?" he asks.

I decide to play along. "I guess one thing leads to another."

"How exactly? How exactly does one thing lead to another?"

"His drinking leads to an interpretation of long term danger by his wife. She then feels the need to do something about it and so counsels him on his ways. He then feels upset about being counseled and feels compelled to respond by drinking more and so on."

"May I summarize, *action* by A leads to *interpretation* by B, which then leads to a *response* by B. *This response* by B leads to an *interpretation* by A, which then..." His voice trails off as he notices me nodding vigorously. I'm actually waiting for him to get to the point. "Imagine that instead of being a **vicious cycle** it was actually a **virtuous cycle**. An ob-noxious customer contacted you to tell you about a need that they felt you were not fulfilling. Your interpretation of this contact was that of an opportunity to provide enhanced offers to customers. And so your res-ponse was to modify the offer and the underlying business process appropriately. As a result, your cus-tomers were delighted and bought more from you, including the demanding customer, who now knew that they would be listened to and felt encouraged to tell you more about what their needs and wants were, giving you the opportunity to continue to satisfy them before any competitor could get any closer."

The penny drops. I see the point.

You adapt with your customers, you grow with your customers, you co-evolve. If you are in any way serious about *maintaining customer satisfaction* it is essential that any approach you introduce is *adaptive and co-evolves*. You remember the questionnaire you used?

"Yes," I reply.

"When I asked you if you had used the same questionnaire you said yes. If you are co-evolving would you use the same questionnaire twice? Wouldn't you let your customers, especially the demanding ones help you to decide what should be in it?"

I'm beginning to understand why he grinned so aggressively when I challenged him about whether he was making too much of the obnoxious demanding customers. It's true. In a fast changing competitive environment, especially one where new competitors arise who are not our traditional competitors, it becomes critical to keep a co-evolving relationship with our customers. I'm re-drawing all my mental maps. I'm redefining how I think about our customers. I'm silently listening nodding in empathy to keep him talking.

"*Everything has sell-by dates* so if you want to have *an adaptive response* to your customers you must always *loop up* any *interaction* you have *with them*. Try to turn it into a **virtuous cycle**. To really run a customer-focused business you must *be careful which customers you* *choose to be the right customers for you*. Co-evolve with customers who are failing at your own peril. However…"

Although I can hear what he's saying, now I'm not really listening to him anymore. My mind is awash with thoughts, questions, ideas. 'If everything has sell-by dates, then our segments, even if we found them would change. How would we cope with that? I guess that's how co-evolution helps. I guess it also means that we have to recognise that the things we are best at and proudest of will not give us the edge forever'. Franck's voice rumbles in my background as I turn to stare out of the window, past the car park below and at the colored flashes which zip past. One millisecond there, the next, gone and yet flow continuously.

"… of course if you think to be *fair is* to be *equal*, you will find, as you did, that your initial market research was spread thinly across all customers, without any focus on what groups you were interested in, without a focus on what particular needs of key groups of customers really were. Instead of trying to establish which of the few needs/wants no one or few companies supply, so that you can delight customers through specific actions, you would have picked up both easy to satisfy and unappreciated needs…"

"I'm sorry Franck I wasn't with you. I was preoccupied thinking my own thoughts."

He grins, "It's so frustrating!" he begins, "What's the point in knowing all there is to know about…"

I smile.

The Forthe
THE TALE OF THE LOST SELF-DIRECTED TEAM LEADER

G ive me back the good old days when the boss was the boss and there was no question. The days when you had clear direction and we could just get on with the work without hours of interminable meetings. And hours of people discussing the 'process' or arguing over 'ground rules'". I'm expressive, waving both arms vigorously as if conducting an orchestra.

Franck is grinning at me. It's obvious he thinks I'm acting and that I don't really mean it.

"I do," I say, "I really mean it. This team working stuff is complete bunk." The reason for my outburst is that I've spent the bulk of the day arguing over how to share out a rather meager (well not completely meager, but less than last year) bonus between the 23 of us in the team. Why should I have to suffer a lower bonus than last year through no fault of my own? "Why should I have to share my bonus with a bunch of idiots who couldn't find their way out of a brown paper bag!" I exclaim.

"Why can't you guide them? I thought you were the 'Business Liaison Leader'."

"Aah! There lies another problem. It's not a real leadership role. It's an **extended role**," I almost hiss with cynicism. "I mean, what does **that** mean?"

"So you have no influence over the team?"

I sigh, "Not as much as I wish I had. I mean it's really hard to influence the team. I'm never sure if I should or not. It's all so confusing. When we started it all seemed so clear and straight forward."

"Tell me how it started."

"At the top," I reply sarcastically. "Our board decided that we needed to develop the best way to keep the sales team focused on the 'customer's emerging wider needs'. That's another piece of jargon we now all use, as it if actually means something. We were to do this by creating large regional teams made up of, not only sales people but also some technical experts and some others for bulk."

"For bulk," he chortles, patting his own tummy as if it were mine.

"Very funny," I say quickly. "It all seemed to make sense. Our customers were becoming more and more demanding of the whole offer we provided, they wanted the product service and offer to match up. But I guess what made it increasingly difficult to achieve was the fact that each customer seemed to want something different."

"Each customer?" he asks, sounding amazed.

"Well, not each customer. It was more as if they had formed themselves into gangs, or perhaps clubs, yes definitely, describing them as clubs was far closer to reality. Mmm maybe not quite clubs because that makes it sound as if they knew each other and hung out together. It was more as if they had met secretly and agreed common needs." I liked that bit about meeting secretly. So I think did Franck, who allowed a whisper of a smile to play on his lips for an instant.

"When we noticed this, we'd hired some very expensive management consultants, ABF, who'd investigated these groups, or segments as they called them." I remark almost as an aside, "I guess you can charge more per hour if you use jargon like segment instead of describing them as groups. Anyway it made perfect sense to make it as easy for the people who would have to flex what we offered, to be as close together as possible to them. Both by changing the geographic region we covered and by putting all the people together as one team."

Frank nods sagely.

"This is the bit with the twist. Because we'd put the different people from our different functions together, there was a vigorous discussion at the executive meeting, so I've heard," I say, using the word 'vigorous' euphemistically, "on which function should be in charge of this new meta-function. As I understand it, there was a turf skirmish over ownership and reporting lines. The discussion was at an impasse when one of the very expensive consultants suggested that we use, what he described as, 'self-directed teams'. This would solve the problem about reporting lines and at the same time would result in a significant saving in the cost of at least one level of hierarchy. The savings in managerial cost would go a long way towards paying for the transition."

"Sounds like a good idea," he says encouragingly.

"Yeah that's what we thought. In no time the grapevine was full of gossip about who would be in the new self-managed teams..."

"I thought you said you were using **self-directed** teams."

"Self-managed, self-directed, same thing," I say with a shrug. I notice Franck's expression betrays the fact that he thinks that they are different but he lets it pass. "We had to re-apply for our jobs of course, because there were to be fewer managers. It was tough trying to talk your way into a job which hadn't been defined, because at the time we were applying, the teams hadn't formed. I wasn't too worried. I had a good track record and I'm pretty good at selling myself. I decided to go for the job of Business Co-ordinator and Management Liaison, basically because the salary was rumored to be the largest in the team." I laugh as I remember. "During the interview I was asked why I had applied for that job. I said something really pseud and new age about the 'essential dynamic of team culture in focusing and co-ordinating on key performance indicators'. All the while, as I told this lie, I was thinking to myself, 'It's the salary you liar. It's the salary'."

Franck barely smiles at my guffaws. I can tell that he's wanting me to get to the point quickly. I've been indulging myself with my reminiscences. "To get to the point," I say, "Once all the team members were recruited, we were given dates to launch our new teams with a full day meeting and planning session. The entire process was as well co-ordinated as a military operation. It was like a product roll-out. All twelve teams were kicked-off simultaneously. The appointed day came and..." I pause semi-consciously, as the painful memories and emotions hit me full square in the chest. I can only manage one word. A word that to me sums it all up. "Disaster."

"Nothing is that bad."

"It was. I'd... we'd decided that since we were self-directed, there should be minimum amount of presentations with one person hogging the limelight. When I say 'we', I mean me and the other four people with extended roles. It seemed like a good idea."

"Definitely sounds good. *The method must mirror the message,*" he intones as if quoting some mantra.

"And that there should be as much input from everyone as possible. We wanted to encourage discussion."

"The *medium must mirror the message,*" he intones this time. This is all good stuff. How did **you** manage to turn it into a disaster?"

I choose to ignore the jibe. "The day started with some short scene setting and then into an open agenda of topics to consider. It went fine until after the morning coffee break. After the break somehow we seemed to keep getting stuck in circular arguments. Since we were supposed to be self-managed, no one was sure whose job it was to sort out the disagreements. Frustration levels grew and grew until at 11.23a.m. it blew. People started exchanging personal insults. One very experienced sales manager stood up and insulted all of us saying that it was the worst meeting that they had ever attended and that they wouldn't be attending anymore. Each person sparked off at least one other. At the climax, one of our technical experts lifted a chair above his head and threatened to smash it on the table. This finally stunned us all into silence."

"It sounds like a terrible experience," he remarks empathetically. "What do you think went wrong?"

I pause trying to answer. Trying to reflect on what happened and to draw out some meaningful and insightful conclusions. But, like the thousands of times in the past I've reflected on this event, nothing! "I really don't know," I reply slowly and sheepishly. There was nothing I noticed in the earlier behavior which suggested to me that we were about to have a major row."

Franck shrugs in sympathy, raising his eyebrows and shoulders whilst lowering the corners of his mouth. "So when it started to go wrong, why wasn't it stopped?"

"I guess," I say, trying to think fast, "that we weren't sure, I mean *no-one was really responsible for resolving the conflict.*"

This time he just shrugs downwards with the corners of his mouth. "Anyway, it seemed as if some thought had gone into rolling out the new way of working. A budget had been put aside for us to spend time together, team building. I guess I have to give them credit for that," I say reluctantly. "The state our team was in we needed team building, although 'team super-gluing' would have been a more appropriate phrase. Trying to stitch together the shattered pieces," I say, mixing my metaphors.

"Whilst we were in the process of setting up dates, we had a long wait of course because the organization insisted that we use a specific external facilitation company for all the work. But of course, because all the teams had been kicked off at exactly the same time, they were all experiencing the same problems at the same time. So of course there was a long waiting list. We had a month to wait." I think to myself, 'It's funny how it all comes back to me. All the things which only became obvious in hindsight. I keep wandering off the track because each one tells me something intriguing about how we *failed to give ourselves the best chance of organizing ourselves up appropriately to deliver this New World way of working.' 'It's almost,'* I think, *'as if we had done it in exactly the same Old World way we always used.* Why had we decided to roll-out all the teams at once? I guess we were thinking about the efficiency and neatness of it all. I guess we were thinking that people left out would be concerned. After all it was only fair to treat everyone *equally.* We almost needed to *unlearn that we knew how* to get things moving.' I chuckle quietly to myself, 'It's almost as if *unlearning is more useful than knowing'*.

"You still with us?" Franck asks to jolt me out of my daydream and back to reality.

"Sorry, I was somewhere else. Oh yes, I was saying how after the team building activity two members of the team approached me. They both seemed very stressed and unhappy."

"These were two people who worked together?"

"Not directly. They actually approached me separately. I guess what was strange was that they both made the same request. They asked for a confidential discussion. Of course I agreed. One of them was very experienced and the other very junior. What was even stranger was that they both began the discussion with the same request. In both cases the discussion was exactly the same. They started the discussion by demanding to know to whom they reported. I tried to explain that the purpose of having a team was to allow us to work together. *To work together, with the emphasis on getting the work done, rather than on control and reporting lines.* This explanation, for some reason, made them even more distressed. In the end I just had to give up and to tell them that they reported to me for the next fortnight. They both seemed very relieved at this. The more experienced manager thanked me for providing clarity and direction and said, 'You've taken a load off my mind which would allow me to sleep through the night again'. I was amazed by how stressed they seemed to be because they weren't sure who the boss was! And amazingly, truly enough, over the following fortnight the two would appear regularly at my door with documents to sign or approve." I look at Franck expecting him to be as amazed as I am by their behavior. There is no sign of amazement so I feel I need to explain further. "Here's a once in a lifetime opportunity to have some say over your life at work. It's official! We're empowered! We're free to create the future and these two are hankering after remaining dependent? Bizarre!"

But Franck's expression doesn't mirror the contempt I am expressing, for these two wusses, who won't stand on their own two feet. Instead he has a look of compassion. A genuine compassion reinforced by his words. He says quietly, almost sadly, "I guess New World is tough on some people. Not everyone sees nirvana in being self-directed or self-managed."

I consider his words for a short while, trying to make sense of them. I can't make sense of them. To me, **being** your own boss is far superior to **having** your own boss, so I say feigning lightheartedness, "Guess it takes all sorts."

"Some things do," he responds cryptically. "So what happened next?"

"Well, we got to the second all team meeting." I pause.

"Was it as bad as the first?"

"No. Yes. In a different way. For the second meeting we tried to structure the agenda a bit more. We had a list of topics we had to address. Important topics like deciding who was focusing on which customer and so on. It started well but then we seemed to keep getting lost in circular arguments again. Points would be made, re-made, discussed, turned over, disagreed with and made again. It was so frustrating. It was as if, it was as if we were a group of ditherers rather than a dynamic self-directed team. Fortunately it was only a half day meeting, so we managed to survive it without exploding from stress."

"Progress?"

"Of sorts, but it was as if we were wary of showing any emotion at all. Also everyone seemed pretty embarrassed about what had happened the last time. The team building day though, was a great success. The trainers made us do all sorts of exercises including making us lead each other across a busy four lane highway blindfolded!"

"Onward and upward!" he empathizes enthusiastically.

"Yes. After the team building the morale was actually quite good. On the day after, I received five e-mails with comments about how the whole process had cleared the air and given us a solid base for creating our new team. Strangely enough the notes were to me and only copied to about two or three other people, usually the ones with extended roles. I remember thinking how strange that was. Surely with a self-directed team the e-mails should have been copied to everyone in the team?" I laugh hollowly.

Franck grins back. "Did you get anything else out of the team building, other than great team morale?"

"Yes," I reply, "we used the last few hours to do some goal setting. I was actually surprised by how keen people were to accept and often indeed, set themselves very stretching targets."

"These were *individual* targets, were they?"

"Yes," I reply, "of course."

"Help me," he says, "You know you mentioned receiving e-mails copied only to those of you with extended roles?"

"Yes," I reply cautiously. I'm thinking, 'Why is he asking for my help?'

"During your team build, did you discuss why some people had extended roles?"

"No, I don't think so," I reply trying hard to remember what we'd covered that day.

"Can I make a guess at what happened next?" he asks my permission.

"Yeah sure," I say, "go ahead."

"I guess that the next negative thing you noticed was that your team members were duplicating each other's work in certain areas and as a result wasting a lot of your joint resource. You probably also noticed that they were quite happy, no, better to describe it as uncaring, about wasting each other's time. At worst, they would even be derogatory about each other's contributions. The group meetings quickly returned to being full of circular arguments and then, or rather, and now, you've discovered in surprise that your team budget is overspent for the amount of output anticipated and as a result your bonus is reduced." He breaks to get a breath. "Am I right?"

I don't answer immediately. How does he know all this? He's absolutely right. Have I told him this before? Perhaps on the phone when we were arranging this meeting? I think, racking my brains. I don't think so. You know these consultant types. I know Franck describes himself as an educator but, borrow your watch tell you the time and sell you back the watch. I reply with deep suspicion in my voice, "How do you know all this?"

"You told me yourself," comes the reply.

'Aha,' I think, 'so I was right. I had told him.' "On the phone when we were arranging this meeting, right?"

"No. Just now."

I stare at him in disbelief. 'Just now?' Even I, with my difficulty in sticking to the topic would remember if I'd told him all that just now.

"No I didn't," I argue.

"You told me about your over-riding wish to have everyone involved in all the discussions and decisions, you told me that you hadn't discussed why some people had extended roles and you told me that people were set or set themselves individual targets."

I nod confused.

"You see in the Old World, your boss was responsible for you, your actions and what you worked on. You were also accountable directly to your boss for everything you did."

I nod again, 'Common sense,' I think, 'but what does this have to do with his predictive powers?'

"*In the New World accountability and responsibility are not necessarily held by or to the same person*. Think about accountability as more like saying to someone, "*you can count on me to... deliver... do... whatever,*" and then separately think about responsibility as relating to a person or resource. *Responsibility means that you help that person or resource be all it can be.* So if you are responsible for a person, your focus is on helping them to maximize their capability."

"So?"

"*In the New World you can be accountable to one person whilst someone entirely different is responsible for you.* Don't you see," he says slowly, making me feel I'm being dim, "if your team members don't understand the difference between accountability and responsibility they will try to treat you like an Old World Boss. Also you will find that many team members will only work with people with the same skill base as them in their areas of core expertise. Also if they don't understand the difference then they will not be able to see why, in a self-directed team, some people have extended roles."

I still don't get it. I'm honest, I say, "I still don't get it."

"If they don't understand **why** you have extended roles generally two things will happen. Firstly, if they feel that they are empowered and are supposed to be self-directed, they will apply the 'boss' mental map and as a result feel aggrieved that you are trying to grab too much power in what should be a flat team. As a result they will go off and do their own thing without informing you. In fact, they may go so far as to actively keep many of their actions secret. The second variant which is amusing but prevents you gaining the power of being self-directed is that they will use the 'boss' mental map alone. They will ignore the self-directed aspect, seeing that as little more than a faddish inconvenience and instead treat you like a real boss. They will inform you of everything they do, bottlenecking you and themselves."

"That has already happened," I say recalling the requests I'd described earlier.

"But to make life even tougher for you, another New World change will kick into gear. You see in the Old World the 'boss' model was about control, people doing as you say, **you** co-ordinated activities through issuing orders. It was by the way you planned the issuing of these orders that things got done. In the *New World however, because it is difficult to learn faster than the businessphere changes, it makes little sense to manage primarily through control. It is often more effective to manage through co-ordination.*"

"Sure."

"The problem is that the *co-ordination is through sharing information not through issuing orders*. If you didn't discuss why some people have extended roles, this issue wouldn't have surfaced."

I'm thinking hard. I'd always assumed co-ordination was co-ordination. Franck is suggesting that in the New World co-ordination might be more of a two way process.

"Without understanding that co-ordination and control are not the same and that many members of the team can contribute to co-ordinating its efforts, you will find that there is a large amount of duplication in activities. Particularly if some of your team are going off to do things on their own."

I am getting a horrible sinking feeling.

"In addition," he says, "you will find that none of the team members feel that it **is** their role to help to co-ordinate activities so in the larger group they will all try to get their input in without making sure that fellow team member's contributions are fully utilized. For you, the real killer, of not understanding co-ordination and control, is that you will be unsure of when to intervene. You will see things going awry, but you won't know how to intervene and get them back on track in a 'self-directed' way without being seen as being overbearing. So as your discussions turned circular no one, not even you, knew how to step in and stop it happening."

"That is true," I say, "that's really true."

"Of course, in the *Old World*, because of the overarching importance of control as part of the formula for making money faster through improved efficiency, *challenge was seen as disagreement*. So if you challenged what someone else was doing, unless they were a direct report that was tantamount to corporate suicide. In the New World, challenge is a key factor in ensuring that yesterday and today remain different."

"Of course the final thing, which I'm sure you now realise," he says, trying to flatter me or at least stop me feeling such an idiot for missing the obvious, "is that because of the lack of understanding about accountabilities and because of the way in which you set your targets, by individual, there was absolutely no 'glue' in the team. Each expert focused on their own area, they scrambled over each other, like kids playing 'who's the king of the castle?', in a bid to reach the top not realizing that if all the bodies below were of other team members, the whole heap/pile/pyramid doesn't get any higher. In fact, all that happens is that energy is wasted."

It's so obvious. I can see how we kept on time after time, continuously slipping off the very thin path to success. "I guess if we're going to *do this New World thing* we'd better do the lot *in a New World way*," I remark.

<Toodle-do-doo, Toodle-do-doo, Toodle-do-doo, Welcome back to Now!>

Back in the black and white room. The audience coughs, clears its collective throat and relaxes. Another story, another account. Another

New World dream turned nightmare. The audience also glances surreptitiously at its collective watch and then remarks silently to itself with amazement at how quickly the evening is going. Half of the audience starts to feel fidgety knowing that it will soon be their turn to try to keep the others intrigued.

Franck asks if anyone fancies a short break, perhaps picking up a cup of coffee from the machine and bringing it back in so that they can make progress faster. The audience thinks that this is a great idea and shuffles off in search of a collective cup of coffee. While they are gone, Franck scribbles onto the conveniently placed whiteboard the following words:

- *accountability =/= responsibility*
- *New World co-ordination is different; co-ordination =/= control*
- *Challenge =/= disagreement*
- *Forget all the answers – unlearning more useful than knowing.*

And then he shuffles off himself, in search of a large cup of very black coffee.

The Fifthe
THE TALE OF THE GLOBAL COMMUNICATOR

C ould you hold on please, my mobile's beeping." This is embarrassing but it happens all the time, almost on cue every time I start a conversation on a land line, as if by some ancient spell. I reach into my briefcase to retrieve my mobile phone. And of course, just as you would expect, just as I flip up the protective cover it stops ringing. "Sorry about that," I apologize.

"No problem," comes a cool voice, with an accent, down the line. "I'm sorry it's taken me so long to get back to you. I was teaching all day yesterday. How can I help?"

"Franck, I'm sure that you don't remember me but I was on one of your learning programs last year, on creating virtual organizations?" I probe waiting for a response.

"Yes of course I remember you. You were just about to join a new company, I believe, how is it working out?"

"Good and not so good. That's what I was calling about. I remember we discussed communication?"

"Yes?"

"I was just wondering if I could pick your brains, talk to you about any ideas of how to cope with the amounts of information I'm being deluged with."

"Sure but I must mention that I've only managed to make this phone call in a gap in a session. I shall have to be away in exactly twenty six minutes."

"I'm sure it won't take that long. Let me give you some background. My new organization has offices around the globe. Each office is relatively autonomous and is managed as a separate profit center. However, the current strategy is to try to leverage our size by developing a global capacity to respond to some of our larger clients as well as to develop a global brand and positioning. I have the job of integrating our marketing for all the different units."

"Sounds like a big job," he interjects.

I agree instantly, "Demanding. It means I'm doing a lot of travel although my base is still in this country." I try to move on to the reason I called. "Do you know of any good books or articles on managing time, well not really managing time it's more about managing communication. But sort of..." I'm finding it difficult to clearly state my problem.

"Time management isn't really my area," he replies. "Although I have found that it *is rarely the management of time which is the problem*. Often the real reason that you don't have enough time is something else." Then he chuckles. "Actually when I'm in one of my more belligerent moods I will argue that *you can't manage time, all you can do is spend it*. Spend it doing things, thinking, experiencing. It doesn't really matter how hard you try to manage it, a minute happens every minute. I'm not sure I can really help you with this one."

"Well it's not really time management," I say trying to prolong the conversation, "let me describe what happens to me. I'm finding that even in the calmer periods, when I'm not globetrotting, I'm having to get to the office at 7.00 a.m. each day. And when I am actually in my office I spend huge chunks of my time responding to a deluge of information which comes at me from all directions. I mean, typically, in the morning there are about forty e-mails waiting, a dozen faxes, my voice mail to check, and because there is just so much of it unless you respond to it there and then you can't get back to it. So I don't really prioritize, as I was taught as a junior manager, anymore. And then, having just waded through all the stuff sent to me, I have to wander through our organizations groupware for all the non-proactive stuff, and then just as I get the feeling I might be getting on top of it, the post arrives."

Franck bursts into unsympathetic laughter at the other end of the line. "Multi-media-data-deluge!" he chuckles "a common syndrome afflicting managers these days."

"It's a nightmare and because like many modern organizations we've done away with secretaries, I have to manage it all on my own."

"Have to?" he interrupts.

"Yes. Our policy is not to employ secretaries," I explain again. "It's a headcount thing. And you can imagine what a nightmare it is when I travel. I carry a large black bag containing phone jacks for all the countries I visit regularly, along with a couple of spare pcmcia modem cards."

Now Franck is killing himself with laughter. He seems to find my discomfiture extremely amusing. This is not what I had expected. I decide to tell him more so that he can grasp the seriousness of the situation and offer some sober advice.

"I found it such hard work to try to keep in touch around the globe that I even ended up buying a second mobile phone. So I now have two phones which divert to the other on no reply in case one of them is low on juice."

No laughter. I think I'm winning.

"Last month I decided to experiment with video conferencing as a method of reducing my travel load."

"Good idea," he responds without a hoot. "It can be very effective."

"Not for me it wasn't. I'd heard that many organizations do it all the time and swear by it. My experience was the pits. First, it took ages to arrange and book a time when all the people we wanted to interact with would be available. It was as bad as organizing a meeting, no worse because we also had to schedule time on three VC rooms around the globe. The event itself was a bit unruly. In Boston they had auto camera zoom which would swing wildly round their room to focus on the person speaking. It made anyone watching feel sea-sick."

"Couldn't you have *planned* your *agenda* and *selected primary speakers* for each topic to stop the whizzing around?"

"I guess we could have. I know that now. I didn't know that then. I think in retrospect there are several other things we would have done, like for example, *get people to introduce themselves in a brief but interesting, and possibly humorous way*. Not necessarily at the beginning because that slows the start to boredom. But perhaps at intervals. It was only when we were about half way through that I realised that the reason that some of the people, who should have been key contributors to the conference, were being reticent was because they weren't sure what the job roles of some of the faces they were seeing, were. We should have made quite clear what the timings were for each topic and broken up the presentation/discussion format with a few short breaks"

"Nice analysis," he congratulates.

I chuckle, "I guess the funniest thing that happened was that one of the Japanese participants started to fall asleep. You see the time schedule meant that for them it was some horrendous hour of the morning. When it was noticed, it really broke the tension and there were hoots of laughter. One of the participants described it as 'virtual jetlag'."

"Brilliant!"

"Yes but I'm still not sure that we achieved the objective we set out to, which was to resolve some issues and gain commitment for the next phase. By the end of the conference, we had heard all the right noises but I'm not sure that they have really bought in."

"Oh! I didn't realise that you were trying to use cyberspace for handling emotional issues."

"Nor did I," I reply, now starting to understand what the real problem was.

"Tell me about your other stuff, your e- mails in particular, are the messages you receive useful?"

"Are you kidding me? About 5% is really useful and critical, about another 10% is interesting or nice to know but the rest.."

"Garbage?"

"Worse. Garbage with attachments, I really hate those attachments, they take ages to open and half the time they are written in a more recent version of the software ensuring that you can't actually read them."

He giggles.

"The annoying thing is that often, even with all those e-mails, I still have to really hunt and probe to get some of the answers I really need. You see the problem is that our organization is so fragmented that no one is really sure where the power structures lie. So even before we had e-mail there was a lot of CYA activity..."

"CYA?"

"Cover your anatomy."

Now he laughs down the line.

"Now, what you find is that you get copied in on everything. Especially me. When my job was initially announced they made it sound as if I would have influence over the marketing and sales budgets and hence the operational spend budgets of all the operations. People seem to copy me in on everything!"

"Apart from, what was it you called it, CYA, do you have any idea of other reasons people send you this vast tide of cybertrash?"

"No," I say shaking my head forgetting that he can't see me.

"Do you remember our discussion about the Old/New Worlds?"

"Yes."

"In the Old World information flowed up and down the line, the reporting line was the same as the main conduit for information flows. Generally, because what individuals did was closely regulated by their line manager, most information passed was either specifically asked for by the reporting line or was information which had always been gathered and distributed, like sales reports or machine efficiencies."

I say, "Yes," not sure of where this is leading but more to encourage him to keep talking.

"The New World creates three big headaches, for a start because the rate of change is generally faster than the rate of organizational learning, *a lot of the information generated is being produced for the first time ever*, so there is a question over who needs access to it. Also in the New World there is a need to *communicate with other people and stakeholders involved in the overall process or project*. So most of the *information conduits should run along the processes or projects* and not up or down some control 'hierarchy'. Co-ordination is through information not through issuing orders. But the third is even funnier. Because in the New World the learning takes place throughout the organization it is not appropriate to regulate what people learn. But the effect of that, is that the people in the organization become very unsure about which other stakeholders need to have access to what they have learnt. They decide more is better than less and so spray the organization with the data they have collected hoping that all will be well."

"But it's not well," I protest. "Most of the stuff I get sent gets deleted as soon as I look at it."

"Why?"

I think, 'Why is he asking me 'why?' I'd have thought that that was obvious, it's garbage.' I say, "Because it doesn't answer any of my questions or issues, because often I'm not sure what they want me to do as a result of reading their e-mail, because it is often too detailed or general for me to act on and usually because it's too late for me to respond or take any appropriate action."

"Have you told them this?" he asks. "Don't forget that in the most people don't know about the existence of the New World. They think that when they send you some correspondence, any correspondence, it is of value. They don't realise that *information and data are not the same thing*, you want answers, you want information if you are not asking the question then anything they send you is useless to you. It's just data. It's just data you'll bin. They're still living in the Old World where the questions had long been defined and so the bulk of what was circulated answered the questions and was information. They may also not have understood what stakeholders are and assume that because you are senior you are a stakeholder in a process or project, even if you're not. To you it's garbage, to a real stakeholder who was asking the question it's information. *One person's data is another person's information*," he intones, then he pauses and asks, "Do you follow?"

"Yes," I reply, "Of course, and because the New World disrupts the neat and tidy linear reporting relationships creating a web of stake-holder interactions, using e-mail to inform people or to keep a record of what is happening, is impossible because no single person has the whole picture. I guess that's why we introduced groupware. I don't remember it being explained that way."

"Sending people data is expensive stuff. In virtual cyberspace interactions can be with millions. Remember in Meatspace/Touch-space everything you do costs you money but only a few things you do, which the customer likes, bring the money back in. If you imagine that you cc to 30 people, each of whom takes two minutes to open up and read useless data at $100/hr that is $100 gone to money heaven, or wherever money goes when it dies, remember on a 10% margin that is $1000 additional revenue which needs to be generated to cover the cost of resource wasted on e-mail. Or in your case at 80% of 40 e-mails at, Ooh, $500 per hour, I make that about, er, costs of, er, $2500 per week. Frightening isn't it?"

"Yeah, real scary," I respond, too big headed to tell him that he has grossly overestimated my hourly rate.

"That's why you **must** reply to every single one of those e-mails. You really need to reply to explain about communication of infor-mation. Just create a standard reply with the points you made above; that *the message must serve the purposes of the person being communicated* *with, the level of detail* must be *appropriate for the stakeholder* and that the *timing* of the communication *must make it useful* and that they must *anticipate the thoughts and actions* they wish you to carry out and possibly inform you of them."

"Yup," I respond. It makes sense, but I'm concerned that it may seem Franck must have guessed my thoughts because he says, "If you think it appears unfriendly, preface it in some way, as a chain letter or with a reference to some personal goals of your own."

That seems far more attractive to me. I notice that he is speaking faster now. I guess we must be running out of time. I glance at my watch. Just then my mobile starts ringing again. I decide to ignore it and just let it ring.

He says, "I guess the other thing we haven't quite bottomed out is why you have decided to receive your communication through so many channels."

"Well it wasn't really a decision, it just happened."

"How about having your phone calls managed?"

"Headcount freeze," I reply.

"So why can't you go *virtual*. Come up with a solution which has the *effect* of a secretary *without the traditional form*, and hence avoids headcount implications."

"What would that be?" I say. "I can't think of anything." I think it's a ridiculous idea. In order for someone to take my calls there has to be someone. And in order for there to be someone the headcount has to go up. It's not possible unless that someone is me. And that is pointless.

"Why can't you divert your calls to a call center, people who specialize in phone calls? You could think of them as a 'virtual secretary' having the good effects of a secretary without having to physically be in your building and on your headcount."

"Nice idea. I'll give it a go," I say with enthusiasm muted by the fact that I hadn't thought of it myself. As I reflect on the suggestion it becomes apparent that I was assuming that whoever took my calls would have to be employed by us. A real person **inside** our organization. I hadn't considered for a second that I could direct the communication to someone **outside** our organization."

Franck is moving on now speaking significantly faster than he was at the start of the conversation. "It's probably worth thinking about which medium you want to use for which bit of communication."

"What do you mean?"

"Do you try to channel different communication through different channels?"

"I think so," I say. "I try to use the most convenient ones."

"There is a pause, silence down the line. Franck is obviously trying to format his thoughts. He quizzes gently but quickly, "Can I ask you a personal question?"

"Er, Yes."

"When was the last time you wrote a love letter?"

"Good God!" I exclaim, surprising myself as I swear. I wasn't expecting that question. "I can't remember," I say.

"But you've told your other half by phone about such matters recently?"

"Sure," I reply. In my job, being away from home so much, most of my phone calls home are half task and half 'love' phone calls.

"Well, you see, people find it difficult to express and investigate their emotions in a medium in which they are unfamiliar."

"What do you mean?"

"Many years ago people wouldn't speak of love on the phone, but they would write love letters. Letters had been around for a while and we were so used to them as a means of communication, that we relaxed enough to commit to them our emotions and allow them to act as the medium for communication."

I'm thinking, 'So?'

"As you communicate using the plethora of media you have available, you need to give some thought to the emotional content of the communication you are carrying out. Newer media with which we are less familiar often do not allow us to relax enough to move from the communication of logic and facts to the higher order range of emotional conditions. So it's not really surprising that you didn't get complete buy-in with your video conference. The participants' emotions were already tied up, engaged in handling the mechanics of video conferencing, a change from the norm. They were working flat out to assess if this **change** was actually a **threat to their security**. Their emotions were far too busy handling the changed medium to focus on even considering how they felt about your proposal and if they would buy-in."

"I see," I reply. "I hadn't really thought about that."

"But it's worse than that. You see the thinking part of you also needs to be considered. There are some issues which are only understood if there is an interactive dialectic between the people communicating."

"I don't understand," I say bewildered.

Franck chuckles loudly down the phone. "Joke! Ha! OK I know it wasn't very funny but I hoped it would make the point."

"What point?"

"The point that for some things, it is essential to interactively develop clarity of understanding. For some things this is best done with rapid and immediate response otherwise we lose the thread of the argument, we forget the points which were being made and how they fit together."

"Got it," I say, "Video conferencing allows the high rate of interactivity for discussing a complex problem but is not useful for either resolving an emotional issue or getting buy-in. At least not at this stage. At least not whilst it still feels new to people. Is that what you meant?"

There is no immediate reply. "I'm sorry, someone was asking me something this end. What did you say?"

I repeat what I had just said.

"Precisely! You need to consider all your communication routes along with the medium you must use to make the communication most effective. Some media allow you to *operate effectively in the same place and at the same time*, like *meetings*. That makes them particularly *suitable*, especially if people are familiar with them, *for communicating* issues which are both *emotional* and require *immediate interaction* in order to develop understanding. Others, like *e-mail*, have the advantage of *allowing you to interact with other people in different places at a different time* from when you send the communication. But because they are new and because they are not immediate they are far less effective for handling a high emotional content or the need for immediate interactivity. But brilliant at *conveying factual information*, updates and the like. They are very effective when you wish to avoid the 'virtual jetlag' you described before because they *allow time to operate in parallel, not just in series* as it usually does. You see, for communication which is effective even when interaction is not immediate," he says, "parallel time is the trick. Does all that make sense?"

"I think so."

"Good, I'm afraid I have to go now. I have to be somewhere else in Meatspace."

I laugh. "Sure, thanks. It's been very useful."

"Bye."

I barely have time to reply. There's a click and he's gone, leaving my mind whirling with thoughts of sames and differents, virtual secretaries and information without answers.

<Back to the future, swirly wavy lines this time.>

- *go virtual*
- *fair = different*
- *data =/= information*
- *time = parallel*

Bullet points are added to the white board.

"Are we still winning? Do you want to hear more?"

A chorus of 'yesses' and 'uhuhs' follows.

"Great! Who wants to capture our imaginations next?" he challenges.

A hand goes up.

"OK over to you," he says.

The Sixthe
THE TALE OF THE SELF-STARTER'S GROWING PAINS

I guess I might as well give up now.' I think to myself. I've always believed that you are never given a wish without being given the means to make it come true. But I'm completely stuck. It's a complete nightmare.

"Could I have your car keys please?"

I hand over my keys and walk to the 'customer care' area towards the side of the showroom away from the gleaming new cars. I notice the coffee machine and walk towards it to negotiate. I make my selection. A voice behind me, just over my left shoulder, says "Hi". I spin on my heel to see who it is.

"Hi Franck," I say extending my arm to shake hands, "Long time."

"Sure is," he replies not giving anything away.

"Three years," I say with certainty. "It was just before I went it alone and that was three years ago."

"So how's business?"

"Business is good but tough."

"Oh?" he says, his inflection conveying the whole question in a single syllable.

"Well I'm stuck..." I say, then remembering my manners, "Would you like some coffee?"

"Yeah, black, just the poison."

I retrieve my cup and punch in the code for his beverage. Now we are sitting across a gray glass covered table. I've explained the nature of my business. Well, our business, the three partners, and what we're stuck with. "It's a real nightmare. We can't grow anymore, without more resource. But I'm stuck with everything, answering the phone, doing the books, writing proposals, the lot and every time we hire anyone else it turns out to be a disaster. We've been operating FIFO."

"FIFO?" he quizzes. "First in first out?"

"No. Well, that's what **we** call it. We're too small to be able to cope with much disruption. To us it means 'fit in or have sex and travel'. The problem is we keep sending people off on round-the-world cruises, entire ship loads."

Franck laughs.

"I don't understand what goes wrong at the interviews. They seem fine, but then when they come on board they just seem to go off the rails. We find we can't depend on them. And if we do depend on them we end up having sleepless nights."

"What do you try to find out at the interviews?"

"What do you mean? We do all the conventional stuff, history, past achievements, aspirations and so on."

"In a New World environment you may be asking them to do things which are very different from their experience."

"Yes we do but with what we're paying we expect some initiative."

"In that case you need not only to discover what they've done but also how they see into the future and how they act to create it. You see, you can observe their **capabilities** but it tells you nothing about their potential. You may anticipate their **potential** but that tells you nothing about their **attitude**. Invest in learning as much about all three as you possibly can."

"Thanks for the advice. I think we do that bit relatively well but I can't seem to work out why they go off the rails when they join."

"How do you decide who does what?"

"Well we've tried using a standard reporting line but we're a bit small and it seems like overkill. But if we let them loose on their own it becomes untenable."

"Why don't you try splitting what you can count on them to do away from what they are responsible for looking after? That way you can slowly bring them into your core team. For every activity they are accountable for set a joint accountability with one of the partners, that way they rely on you but it is apparent that you rely on them. Slowly the team forms and builds."

"G1FOX" a voice calls from the reception desk.

"That's me!" responds Franck and rises to retrieve his car.

He turns over his shoulder to say "That way you can also treat them as if they are learning, which is what they are doing, whilst treating the other partners as if they know what's what."

I can see the sense in what he is suggesting.

"Makes sense," I reply.

A mechanic pulls up outside in a kingfisher blue coupé. Franck turns, shakes my hand and says apologetically, "I have to be somewhere else. Tell me," he asks as he holds the door open for the mechanic, "do you really have to employ these people directly?"

"What do you mean?" I ask.

"I guess the other option you have is to *go virtual*." With that he smiles and glides off gracefully in his blue chariot.

<present... past... present... past... present... present... >

One of the participants comments, "Short, sweet and to the point. What do you mean 'virtual', Franck?"

Franck shrugs and offers, "Could I explain tomorow?" he continues to make notes on his board:

- *go virtual*
- *fair=different*
- *split accountability and responsibility.*

The Sevenf Tale
THE STRATEGIC CHANGE IMPLEMENTER'S TALE OF PARADOXES

S o now I can't go back and tell the SMG that we got it all wrong," I say.

We're sitting in Meeting Room 5. Meeting Room 5 faces inwards, towards the atrium twelve floors up. Ceiling-to-floor glass gives it an open feeling. It provides a panoramic view of all that goes on on the floors opposite. Also at this time of day, it receives a splattering of natural light from the skylights above. Because of all this, it is easy to forget, once in Meeting Room 5, that from the rest of the building you resemble a goldfish in a tank. This goldfish tank is currently shared by one of my colleagues, Nige and a visitor, a man with a broad back, a broad smile and an amusing accent.

"Not all!" protests Nige.

"Well it feels that way," I insist.

The visitor clears his throat. "Well it seems to me as if you've started a number of things. And I guess you started them in good faith. The SMG?..."

"Senior Management Group," I explain.

The visitor continues. "The SMG should be able to understand that. Let's see *how it all came about*. So, why don't you try explaining to me what you've done so far and why, and then perhaps we can work out a way forward together."

I look at Nige. He stares back and then he rolls his head from side to side as if to say, 'Maybe, OK, we could give it a go'. I interpret that as a "yes" and launch into an explanation. "Well perhaps I should tell you some background. Our organisation is trying to maintain its competitiveness. One of the routes we are taking is to look at our IT capability. It has become increasingly obvious that IS/IT can function either as a source of competitive advantage or act as a tremendous barrier."

Franck nods eagerly. I can see he thinks it's a normal problem for organizations. I want to impress on him the differences in our situation.

"For us it's more a matter of life or death. The faster and more effectively we can implement IT/IS solutions the more business we can do and the better it is for returns."

Nige chips in, "You see we are now almost completely dependent on IT for running our business. And in addition we need the IT systems to be able to effectively audit what's going on so that we can present a clean bill of health to the Regulator. Without the ability to be able to say we know what's going on in our business, the Regulator hovers, keen to shut down any operations which look even slightly dubious. It's all hyper sensitive now." He refers to a recent scandal which was given an ultra-high profile by the media. "What is particularly annoying is that meeting the Regulator's requirements always raises our cost base, rarely ever making us more money. It's really important that we get solutions to these externally imposed conditions as cheaply and as quickly as possible."

Now Franck is nodding slower and more thoughtfully. He is obviously getting the picture. "So, actually getting working solutions is a major problem?"

"Yes," I reply, "but not the only one. The market keeps changing. Opportunities arise very quickly and then disappear again. We have some very tight windows in which to make a decent margin. Often, no-one has the slightest idea how to take advantage of the opportunity presented. Also, the business is now fully global and yet we develop and create European solutions, American solutions and Japanese solutions. Three times the cost for smaller markets."

"And we all make the same mistakes," quips Nige, "but keep them to ourselves allowing the other divisions to repeat our mistakes."

Franck looks deep in thought now. He is obviously hooked.

"And remember I mentioned the Regulator?" I ask. "Well, they just keep up creating more and more elaborate processes for us to comply with. In fact the arbitrary imposition of compliance rules is one of the biggest unknowns in our overall planning cycle."

"Sounds bad," Franck comments empathetically.

"It is," responds Nige flatly.

"Well we figured that to be *successful in business in the future* we needed to *make sure that our projects and change initiatives* were *implemented* and *implemented fast around the world*. In order to achieve that we thought it would be best *to select and impose a single unambiguous approach* on all the people accountable for delivering the change and then to *control it rigidly."*

"Sounds like one way of doing it," comments Franck non-committaly.

"Sure, but I guess our only worry was that the projects were all different. Some we could plan for, others simply arose as the year went on, but we could cope because they were similar to past projects. And with others they appeared out of the blue and no one had the faintest idea what to do or even how to start to tackle the issue. So it also seemed that in order *to have a successful business in future* we needed to use as much as possible a *planned directional approach* but we *also* needed to have the *ability to evolve approaches and solutions*. So whilst on the one hand we were keen on single approach, this other pressure meant that we should instead *develop flexible methods* and *allow the project leaders to select and control* the best route."

"And that's another," he comments with a wicked laugh.

"At the time we were under tremendous pressure to deliver some of the outstanding projects. Our group head was so concerned about the fact that two thirds of our projects were running over time or money that he was having difficulty sleeping. What made it worse for him was that we didn't actually have an effective way of keeping him up-to-date on what was actually happening, so whenever he heard about a project over run it was in the past and there was nothing he could do except try to deal with the implications and consequences."

"Yes," adds Nige "and he was always the last to know. It was as if all the project managers knew the adage, 'Don't tell the boss bad news'. He was the boss, so they avoided telling him bad news. So the clients, the main business, would always know first and get their attack in before he was expecting it."

"Poor guy."

"You should have been here to see him age. He was in his mid-forties but he looked about sixty," Nige observes unsympathetically.

"Yes. It was terrible. Anyway, the Turin Project exploded on him. That tipped the balance. We decided to go the route of a single approach. We asked a consultancy, Aptitude Inc. Have you come across them?"

"I've heard of them," Franck says. "Big in Construction I think."

"Anyway, we asked Aptitude Inc. to propose us a method. And the rest is history," I say, picking up a fat lever-arch binder containing millions of forms and checklists."

"But why is this a problem?"

"I guess my real worry is that it has cost us a small fortune for Aptitude Inc. to interview our people, thirty of our people to be precise, and design and tailor their methodology. And with what you told us in the first fifteen minutes of our meeting they are simply selling us a standard package, which is centuries old and we are already discovering is far too rigid for the wide range of projects and changes we are trying to implement. All the project leaders with the more challenging projects are refusing to follow the methodology. They say it's unhelpful and that they can't complete many of the forms. How do I explain away the poor return we've managed from that piece of work?"

"Sorry, by challenging you mean?" Franck lets his question hang in the air.

"The projects with the less clear and obvious terms and conditions. Not the repeats. The awkward ones, usually the ones we make really big bucks on."

"So you have selected a methodology which only applies to the repeat projects."

"I guess so," I reply compliantly.

"Why?"

"What?"

"Why do you think you ended up choosing an approach best suited to the projects which make you less money? The more **closed** ones where the outcome and the method are well understood by all involved? Why do you think that you opted for a methodology for those rather than for the more **open** ones, the sort where you were either unsure of what you were trying to do or how you were trying to do it?"

"I guess the consultants must have suggested it."

Franck looks at me, his eyes fixed, like a bird of prey on its midday meal. It's obvious he thinks I'm passing the buck.

Nige isn't very helpful. He chips in, "I don't think so, I think we asked them to focus on that sort of approach."

"Well," I say, "it seemed like a good idea. Things were moving very fast in the market and we had to make some headway as quickly as possible." I explain, "You see, *in order to match the pace of change* and diversity of change of our customers and competition, it seems that we must *deliver* quickly tangible clearly **controlled** and directed *change*. This means that we *must encourage* the implementation of *closed projects*, change initiatives in which we **know what** to do and **how** to do it. On the other hand, in order to *match the pace and diversity of change* forced upon us by our customers and competition, we must explore widely delivering improvements, which may only become attractive as we observe them. We must be able *to stick with intangible emergent deliverables*. That infers that we *must encourage open projects*," I say using Franck's expression. "Changes where we either **do not** completely **know what** to do or **how** to do it."

"It seems to me as if each time you've talked yourself into an either/or position and then taken one option, whole. No modification. And no paradox busting."

Nige replies before I have a chance. "I can see that. I guess it's because we were under too much pressure."

"Now who's making excuses?" I comment, adding, "I guess the other bit, which I haven't mentioned is that Aptitude Inc. had also used the interviews as assessment centers. They have recommended certain people as real material for making Project Leaders, pay, grade-scale and all that."

"Uhuh," Franck responds.

"Well the problem is that the people they've shortlisted, how can I put it? The people **they** see as 'real' Project Managers seem to be the ones... Let me say they've ignored other people we could have put on the list. The ones who always make something good happen, no matter how open the brief."

Franck shrugs. "Well what do you expect? If change comes in different types and your consultants have only concentrated on closed change, they will probably have selected those who are very efficient at 'painting by numbers'. Not surprising that they've ignored the others."

"I guess what he's trying to confess to," adds Nige "is that Aptitude's recommendations leaked and now we've upset one half whilst delighting the other half. And yet to succeed we will need **all** of them to play to their strengths."

"I couldn't have said it better myself," congratulates Franck. "I guess what we need to do immediately is to get everyone, as quickly

as possible, to understand the two paradoxes but even more important to understand the full spectrum of change we find in the New
World. We need them to grasp the full range from closed, almost
painting by number type activities, where options are closed and we
fully understand what to do and how to achieve it, to opportunities for
us to apply our capabilities to new objectives, through implementation
quests, with clear objectives but no clarity in how to achieve the goal,
through to the totally baffling, unclear **fog**gy projects. We need to
help them understand how their contribution adds to the whole." He
pauses. "If we can get the SMG to understand this as well, we may
find that they see all of it as success. "

"Yes," I reply, delighted at seeing a way forward, "I guess we do."

"I think the other thing we'll also need to look at is the stake-
holding in each project. We'll need to reverse the situation where one
of the key stakeholders was actively kept in the dark on the negative
aspects. We need to make your people recognise that at the end of the
day it is the stakeholders, all of them, who decide whether a change
has succeeded or failed."

"Great idea," I say supportively, "So what do we do next?"

<I guess I have to drag you back into the present again.>

This time the following words go up on the white board:
*   *and!*
*   *paradox busting*
*   *modularise*
*   *clarify your stakeholders*
*   *focus*
*   *fair = different.*

The Aigthe Tale
THE ORGANIZATIONAL DEVELOPER'S DIMENSIONS

S o we'd come to the conclusion that we would have to re-organize again. That would make it the fourth re-organization in two years. I'm not sure we could get away with it without everyone else in the organization deciding that we'd lost the plot."

"I see," he responds neutrally.

"When we redrew the organogram, erm, organization chart," I explain, "the lines were everywhere, very confusing, so we had to simplify it down and the final structure has lines to different places so re-organization is what is being suggested."

"Mmm," he hums non-committaly

"If I'd known that trying to make the organization more agile would have resulted in another re-organization, I wouldn't have bothered."

"Why, what were you expecting?"

"Well I'd assumed that being more agile meant that we could overcome the organizational tensions and be quick to respond. Re-organizing takes a long time. It is also very unproductive and a corporate morale buster. It's a nightmare to make it work because it is very difficult to get buy-in into any re-organization across the organization. I mean if you want to re-organize, do you *involve the people who are to be re-organized in the analysis and discussion?* If you do there is a fair chance that you hand them all the ammunition they need so that they get what they want out of the re-organization. This is not always the same as what the organization needs. So before implementation you need to assert what the organization needs and as a result there is a head-to-head and the inevitable falling out with some people disgruntled and others delighted. Net result, no buy-in across the board. On the other hand you can *lock yourself away, with a really trusted small group or perhaps a bunch of consultants.* Beaver away at re-aligning resources and reporting lines. Whilst you are doing this the level of distrust grows exponentially and also the rumor mill gets going. Everyone stops work waiting for the outcome. You announce the new structure. If it's a small change, then the 'So what?' attitude kicks in and no one takes any notice of the changes and things carry on more or less as they were previously. Or worse, the change is the significant and dramatic change which actually needs to occur. The surprise element induces denial and fear and often paralyses people rather than spurring them to action. Net result, no buy-in into the re-organization."

Franck laughs out loud at my description of the re-organization process. We are in a 110 seater hall where I have just attended a breakfast meeting. We are sitting on the edge of the stage. Around us is the din and clatter of plates, cups, saucers and crockery being gathered up by the restaurant staff. Dressed in black and white they scurry around in a purposeful but apparently disorderly manner, like ants clearing up their nest after a rainshower. Behind us the stage crew are also active dismantling all the equipment used in the talk. "You will often find," he says, "that in the Old World people saw re-organization as the one and only route to re-aligning resources. Re-organization actually works most effectively in situations where the processes which the resources are assigned to, are clearly understood and the resources actually have the capability to operate in a re-aligned format. Otherwise re-orgs are merely destructive. I call this the Petronius Paradox..."

"Petronius Paradox?" I quiz.

"I stole it from one of the oldest quotes on re-orgs around. It's from a geezer named Gaius Petronius. Apparently, centuries ago the Roman empire had a similar Old World New World split." He is referring to the model he has been presenting during the breakfast meeting. "Apparently there was really rapid change, at least for them and their institutions, so I understand," he says wryly. "Gaius was a middle manager. Job title Centurion?" His voice rising with a slight inflection at the end of the sentence. "He said something like, 'We trained hard to meet our challenges but it seemed as if every time we were beginning to form into teams we would be re-organized. I was later to learn that we tend to meet any new situation by re-organizing. And what a wonderful method it can be for creating the illusion of progress while producing confusion, inefficiency and demoralization.'"

I laugh. I've heard the quote before but I hadn't realised where it had come from. "Too true," I concur.

"So why does this same thing happen over and over and over?"

I shrug, "Life, human nature, I guess."

Franck isn't going to let me get away with a superficial answer like that. He presses me for a better answer. "No, seriously, why does the same thing happen over and over again?"

I try to answer seriously, "I don't really know. I mean all through my career everywhere I've worked at some time has been re-organized at least once whilst I've been there. Years ago when I started in business the company would spend about two years planning the re-organization. The implementation took a while and then they would live with it for about a decade. These days it seems to be fortnightly." I exaggerate for effect.

He smiles.

"No. I honestly don't know," I say.

Franck changes his line of attack. "Have you ever seen an effective re-organization?"

"No, not really. I remember in one company we allowed the shop floor workers to rearrange their handovers and the groups in which they worked in order to match more effectively what had become a very unpredictable and peaky demand pattern for certain products. Mmm, that worked a treat, but it wasn't really a reorganization because the management structure wasn't changed."

Franck is staring at me, eyebrows raised. Like a hawk on its final descent to lunch. "So what you are saying is that the only time you've seen an effective re-organization was when the actual pattern of the work people do changed, although the management structure remained the same?"

"I guess so." The irony of what I said is now slowly starting to dawn on me.

"Any conclusions about what makes an effective re-organization?"

"I guess where all that changes is reporting lines, often nothing really results. Nothing **really** changes."

"But in the past, why did you change **only** the reporting lines?"

Again I'm stuck. 'I don't know why,' I think. "Isn't that how it's done? I mean, I know how a re-org is done."

" I wish you didn't," he responds surprisingly brightly.

"You wish I didn't?" I say, repeating his comment.

"If you didn't know how to do a re-org you might have questioned a couple of the assumptions you were making a bit more closely."

"I don't understand."

Around us the clatter of crockery has died down and yet there is still furious and frenetic activity. Franck looks up at the black and white figures scurrying around. I follow his gaze. "I wonder if they know how to clear the room. They must have done it a thousand times. I wonder if they always do it the same way. As long as they **know** how to clear up a room there is no real innovation. *Innovation only comes from not knowing.*"

I'm beginning to understand his point about re-orgs.

"Within an organization all the knowledge is spread about, little bits in each person's brain. Changing how we organize ourselves is difficult because we have to change how the work actually gets done. To achieve this, many people have to forget what they know and together, jointly, invent something new, something that they didn't already know."

I get the point. "Got you," I say.

"That," he says, "that and the fact that two of your other assumptions are completely wrong."

I think, 'What assumptions? What does he mean, I'm completely wrong?' I say, "I don't follow."

"In the New World you can't effectively represent all the things which are important to business success on an organization chart. You told me that in the only really effective re-org you had seen, hand overs changed, who was doing what for whom changed and yet the management reporting lines stayed the same?"

"Yes."

"So what you are explaining is that the people you count on to do the work, the accountabilities, are not the same as the information flows which say what is being done."

"Yes?" I say this time with less certainty.

"And it is possible that the people who are responsible for making sure that the resources were available, the managers, are not necessarily lined up with the outcome of the task to be carried out?"

I pause trying to work it out.

"That must be true because you changed the work and who did what without reshuffling the managers and yet the managers retain responsibility for the availability, but not the deployment of the resources."

"Er, yes."

"So in this case we can't assume that the *reporting lines* tell us anything at all. They *don't line up with the accountabilities or the information flows* but only with the responsibility for resources."

"So?"

"There are too many elements in the New World structure you are trying to operate."

I'm still puzzled. Franck's explanation isn't helping.

He can obviously tell from my glazed look that I am not following.

"In an Old World environment, the focus was on efficiency, more of the same with greatest knowledge and experience held in few places, a few heads. Those were the places to which information had to flow. Those were the places all decisions were made. The actual under-lying processes, the actual work people did was far less important than ensuring that information and control resided with the decision makers. It made good business sense to develop a process, chop it up into specialist areas, divisionalize, and keep each specialist area reporting separately on the efficiency of their part of the operation. Few people required the information on the whole picture and few people made decisions."

I'm still thinking, 'So? Everyone knows that we need to empower people more, big deal.' I say more politely, "Yes, I understand that."

"Because of those conditions you could control almost everything through a linear hierarchical structure. Route information flows along the same management channels as accountability and responsibility. And throw all the others in as well: the career track, office size, pay structures, and so on. Neat. Tidy. Efficient. Everything fits, shoe-horned into a simple, self-similar structure, the reporting line."

I nod vigorously. He is telling me nothing new and I'm trying to encourage him to get to the point.

"But what do you do if in fact it becomes *better business to split the routing where decisions were made* – who does the work, where information flows to and how it gets there? What if you would rather have pay structures which are not linked to the number of people reporting to you but instead to scarcity in the market or utilization of a particular skill or even behavior, for example, leadership? If you stop assuming that the 'ones at the top' are the only sources of leadership? What then? Then you need to rethink the building blocks. The diagram you would choose to draw to represent, say information flows will not be the same set of lines as for accountabilities. Do you think this is why you ended up with such a complicated initial organizational chart?"

Now I think of it, Franck could be right. The reason our chart looked so complex was because we were trying to represent all the elements he described, onto the same diagram. I say, nodding, "Maybe."

"How many different elements, dimensions do you think you need to consider representing in order to explain your agile organization?" I know the answer is more than one. We have already discussed three, and my intuition tells me that by the time we've considered customers and how to structure to focus on their needs, by the time we've worked out how to keep our skills and capabilities up and made sure we don't break regulations, there will be at least a couple more. I say, "Probably a lot."

"*A lot. Each element on its own is simple. Each element separately needs attention, focus and design. But together they form a structure complex enough to handle all the challenges of the New World environment and yet not be complicated, or else we lose all the agility we seek.*"

"Yeah that makes sense," I say, trying to work out how we've now reached a conclusion which looks so obvious only in hindsight.

And then he asks, "Do you still think you can adequately represent the New World organizational structure in two dimensions on a sheet of paper?"

"No."

"So tell me," he says, his voice slowing and dropping in pitch, "Why are you reorganizing in two dimensions, redrawing your line structure, to meet a demand for something which will never be explainable in two dimensions?"

I smile. I understand. I say, "We can't ever win with re-organization as a method can we?"

"Only in the very short term. In the long term you may find it more effective to create natural work groups and structures which exist to deliver what you need when you need, having the effect you desire but without the traditional organizational structures, virtual structures. You will also want to think about your information flow channels and think about how to use the modern information technology to enable you to run such complex structures without them becoming too complicated." He glances at his watch purposefully signaling that our discussion is at a close.

He's right, perhaps I do *need to unlearn things, perhaps everything*. If we are going to build effective complex organizations from simple units I'm going to need to establish what the simple units for my organization are. I smile relishing the challenge. Delighted that I may be able to avert yet another re-organization I say, "Thanks, I think breakfast is finally over."

< Amazingly, in a flash, time whizzes by back to the present. We miss the end of Franck's short discussion with the group. All that appears to have changed is the whiteboard, which now says:>

- *responsibility and accountability*
- *must work in two dimensions*
- *complexity and complication are NOT the same*
- *unlearn everything*

The Ninthe Tale
THE TALE OF THE INFORMATIZED MANAGER

To: Franck@pombasher.com
Date: 25th Jun
Re: Information issues

You may recall giving me your e-mail address last week and saying I
should contact you if I have any further thoughts or ideas.
I really enjoyed the conference, especially your session on
'Organizational Magic'. I felt that you made some powerful points
during the session but there are some areas I wasn't too sure about.
Also I wanted to discuss in more detail our company's attempt to
become all modern and to introduce e-mail and groupware to all its
operations world-wide. We've had some difficulty getting it to
provide us with real value. True, we have made it to the stage
where we can no longer remember what life was like before e-mail,
but there is far too much of it and our current experiments with
shared databases and groupware don't seem to be working. Do you
have any experience of this sort of problem?
i

To: i_formatised@org.co.uk
Date: 25 Jun.
Re: Information issues

You need to tell me more about why you are implementing e-mail
and groupware. Why for?
F

Our company has grown significantly over the past five years and
now we are a significant global player with operations in 40
countries. It has now become too difficult to manage all our

operations via phone and face to face meetings. Also, we felt that we might gain some strategic synergies through shared information and knowledge management. We felt it was important to signal the importance of the move, by hooking up all employees at once and also by making an appropriate investment in common platforms and systems. We used the approach of lowest common denominator, with local and individual customisation. The expense was significant but we felt it was important enough. We had to gain approval from our shareholders for reduced returns for the current year. We also felt it would allow us to provide effective links to the Internet and through that we would be able to market our products and provide relationship support for our customers.

Does this make sense?

i

Yes. Sure. I can see that you had very good reasons for doing what you've done. What's the problem?

F

We are being completely swamped by a tidal wave of information. Everyone seems to be spending about an hour a day opening e-mails about cars in the car park with lights left on, and about the leaving parties of people on the other side of the world. It's unbelievable and the information which you do get sent which is of some relevance, is hidden away in attachments which take five minutes to open. The shared databases all quickly seem to become rambling and too big, more like trash bins than accessible databases. We've tried asking people to be more focused but with no real result. And many key people still don't use it. And the final problem, it's killing the buzz in the office. People are sending e-mail to guys they sit next to.

i

Sounds like three problems. People are posting information which is of no use? Some people refusing to play and there seems to be inappropriate use?

I guess the information one will come with time but the other two might be happening because your introduction of e-mail wasn't robust.

F

What do you mean robust?

i

When you play out a strategy like that, you need to work out whether it is still a good strategy, even if things don't turn out as expected. How could you have organized your electronic communication (I'm not saying e-mail anymore) to prevent people from putting things in the wrong place, or overfilling areas?

Use e-mail when only one person needs to know and there is no further discussion or development of ideas or someone needs to be actively alerted to a problem. Use groupware in all other cases. Because it is passive, you only get the information when you seek it. It is far less intrusive.

Groupware works best when you structure it around the issues that are of interest and give each person the capability to start a discussion or database on a new topic. This stops the rambling you described. Within each database on an issue, have at least four sections. One explaining the purpose of the discussion and any expected outcomes, a frequently asked questions (faq) area, a free format area, a conclusions and actions area.

You also need to find some bait for the guys who aren't logging on. I used to put a copy of the best joke I'd heard that week at the bottom of each e-mail I sent out.

F

ps   attachment is picture I thought you would find amusing.

Nice ideas but how do I do it? And some of these guys are really senior. And you forgot to suggest anything about the buzz.
i

Don't miss the buzz. If it was fun, it will come back. If it was just whitenoise from the hassle of communicating, it won't.
With the senior guys you've got to work out which belief is getting in the way. Some of them believe you can't have an honest conversation electronically. Spend time with them, ask them how they would like to see it being used. If the belief getting in the way is about 'how' things should be done, rather than 'what' should be done, don't worry, it will only be a matter of time and bait. If the belief is about 'what' you will need to modify your strategy to get them on board.
Let me know how you get on.
F
By the way, did you hear the one about...

<Screeching brakes, whirly flashing lights and stuff.>

"So what did happen?" asks the Strategist.
"It worked eventually," replies the Informatized manager.

- *Robust or bust*
- *fair = different*
- *reinvent information*

The Tenf Tale
THE MERGED CHIEF EXECUTIVE'S TALE

T he problem with mergers is that they are like arranged marriages between two lovers. Each of whom is in love with someone else."

"… Please pass your message. hshshsh"

"Alpha Foxtrot Victor Bravo Sierra is an R22 out of Camberley heading for Battersea. Currently over Windsor at Two Tousand Tree Hundred Feet. Request Special VFR to fly H9, H4 and H3."

"hshshsh Squawk 4506 and report over Teddington Lock."

"Will report over Teddington Lock. Bravo Sierra."

"Sorry, you were saying?"

"I was saying that mergers are sent to tempt us with fast returns and saddle us with a huge uphill task."

"I thought you'd promised not to talk about work."

"Well we're not there yet so it doesn't really count does it?"

"I think you've done a great job. I mean three months on and you have a functioning organization. Most mergers don't have a functioning organization sometimes up to three years later. Yours has been almost a textbook case."

I ignore the praise. "We still have lots to do. It seems the faster I push the slower it goes somehow. I mean, I know that most people are very tired. It's been a long slog but somehow the buzz is missing."

"What do you mean?"

I'm not really sure, so I don't reply.

He persists, "Tell me, from your point of view what **has** happened and what **is** happening?"

"Well we worked our way through the standard merger task forces, seeking out the best processes and approaches from each company. We put in place the new account-abilities and responsibilities, around our flattened organizational structure. Most of that has worked but now we are having to deal with a whole ton of small operational irritants, like the e-mail that doesn't work across all our sites, office moves and infrastructure not functioning. At a higher level we are having to redevelop procedures for things even as simple as car booking. Most people are finding it hard to accept and learn the new methods. All this takes time. Meanwhile we are being bombarded by constant requests for reports and information from head office. People are stretched but I worry that they are too stretched."

Franck has a faint smile playing on his lips, "It all sounds typical."

"It may be typical," I say with my usual impatience, "but what can I do to fix it now?"

"Well, you say they are fully stretched?"

"Over stretched."

"So they can't cram any more in?"

"No."

"So what do you think they should do?"

"I guess that they are going to have to prioritise"

"Definitely," says Franck, "*But focus them on the money*. If an activity isn't either part of a money making process or capable of making money on its own they should be trying to drop it."

"I'm not sure that will be enough. I still think they will be above 100%."

"In that case they also need to start *folding their time*, using the same period of time for more than one activity at a time, reusing reports for one head office department with another. Preparing internal reports whilst gathering information for head office. Making sales trips in pairs so that they can continue coaching and mentoring each other, anything at all they can think of."

I'm still not sure that will be enough. I say, "Hmm".

"I guess the other thing for you to do is to encourage them to *unlearn everything*. They need to build new ways of doing things. New ways, over and above the best practice of either original organization. Remember, this is a much bigger organization. Unless they can un-learn everything they will keep trying to make their old learning fit."

"How do I do that? Do I just tell them?"

Franck doesn't reply. He is making a call.

"Alpha Foxtrot Victor Bravo Sierra at Teddington Lock."

"Please report Battersea."

"Will report Battersea, Bravo Sierra," and as if it was a continuation of the call says, "you may need to get them to learn new processes just by getting them doing. Forget communication. Find where it really hurts due to stretch, find the stakeholders, and go. As they change the processes, they will learn about the new organization."

I think about his comments silently for a while.

"Alpha Foxtrot Victor Bravo Sierra at Battersea switching frequency to Battersea radio on 112 decimal 7. Good-bye."

Now we are on the ground and headed for the main terminal. I say, "Thanks. I promise from here on, no more work."

<Can't think of anything humorous.>

- *unlearn everything*
- *show me the money*
- *folding*
- *stop communicating*

The Elevenf Tale
THE RE-ENGINEER'S QUEST

T wo and a half million spent on consultants' fees, and a staff satisfaction survey you'd want to bury. That's the outcome of our re-engineering program. That plus some savings. But given the fact that the customers are still not satisfied with what we offer them, and that our competitors are still hot on our heels, with my hand on my heart I wouldn't describe it as a **complete** success. In fact, we are now actively looking at other initiatives such as Business Renewal to help us because we feel that the business is still at risk."

"I still don't understand it. Re-engineering was the way out of the recession wasn't it? Radical redesign was the obvious thing to do. At least it seemed that way at the time. I must tell you one of the most depressing things I've heard recently was a radio program in which one of the leading Gurus on re-engineering agreed that it hadn't produced the promised benefits and what was more he blamed us, blamed the companies, us the implementers, for not doing it right. I was pretty angry I can tell you. I simply did what I was supposed to. I followed the book. I followed the consultants advice. So how did we get to this unfortunate point?" I know that my voice has risen in pitch and is quivering slightly. I'm uncomfortable about showing too much emotion at this early stage.

"When we began it all seemed so simple. The goal was to try to *make money using the best business processes.* That meant we could either *capture the best of the present* and then build upon it. Or we could create something entirely new. We could *develop a vision with* all the *stakeholder* groups who would be *affected* by re-engineering and then create it. The only slight wrinkle was that business was tough. We were finding it difficult to maintain sales volumes, so few senior exec-utives believed that creating something new would yield the financial results we wanted quickly enough, so when it came for us to start work there was a set of discussions about whether we should capture the best of the existing or develop something new. "You see," I say almost imploringly, desperately hoping that he will understand my dilemma, "to capture the best of the existing meant that *we should put* *significant effort into **studying** how **the existing processes** worked.* On the other hand to create something new suggested that the last thing you wanted to do was to study the existing. Indeed studying the existing would simply lock you into an older set of ideas which would limit your creative possibilities. So that suggested that *we should **not study** the **existing processes***. I must confess I was in the second camp. The discussions were heated. You see, our organization had built its reputation on efficient and persuasive sales force supported by comprehensive service. Anything to do with sales or service tended to be sacred. The discussion did not last very long. We called in a reputable consulting company which had extensive experience in re-engineering and asked them their thoughts. They seemed clear that the route forward was to map the existing processes. They told us that this would give us early involvement from our staff which would be a good thing and would encourage buy-in. And that was it, so we started."

Franck interrupts, "By 'started' you mean you started work investigating the existing processes?"

"Yes," I reply quickly. I'm starting to get into my stride now. I hadn't anticipated how much fun it would be telling this story. There was tremendous energy. Zillions of workshops facilitated by the consultants and a huge budgetary overspend on yellow sticky notes.

"The phase of mapping took a while. It took a lot longer than I had anticipated. It seems that it is quite difficult to know the level of detail at which to stop."

Franck raises his left eyebrow slightly indicating that he doesn't understand.

"You see," I say, and then, "imagine you were mapping out our conversation; now would you write 'speak to Franck' or 'say a sentence to Franck' or 'say one word to Franck and then another word' or 'open your mouth or breathe in and then out letting air flow over your vocal chords etc'."

He nods. "I see," he says slowly. "Carry on."

"There was a downside of interminable discussion about where to stop but there was an upside too. Lots of people saw the process as an opportunity to walk us through their jobs and how important they were so we got a lot of interest from the workshops. Everyone wanted to include all the detail of their jobs. I guess you could think that they were trying to be helpful but another part of me says that there was simply a lot of job justification going on. Many people would describe each alternative scenario that they had to deal with day-to-day as a separate process! By the time we had finished it was obvious that there were about 13 major processes with five levels of sub processes. By the time we had finished it was also obvious that we had spent most of our budget."

"Spent on?" asks Franck for clarification.

"On fees, booking off-site locations for workshops, and on reprographics for neatly drawing up the processes."

He nods. "And had you learnt anything from all this spending?"

"Yes, No, Not as much as we would have hoped. But the consultants certainly had. They had accumulated a ton of what they called 'fact packs'."

He grins. "So what happened next?"

I continue, "We felt under pressure to do something with it all fast, to create some quick wins. To demonstrate that we were making progress. So we held a review and brainstorming workshop. We spent three hours dreaming up ideas of how we could alter the process. It was really good timing because a couple of days later I was asked to make a presentation to the board on progress and what our new processes looked like."

"I presented the work we had done on mapping, showing how convoluted some of the paths were. I told them about a particular document which went through 26 peoples' hands before finally being filed. There was a good response. And then I presented one of our ideas for completely altering the way in which we carried out sales. It eliminated most of current practice. The approach we proposed automated many of the activities we currently did and relied on using a complex relational database. We called it a breakthrough project."

Franck repeats, "A relational database?" making it clear that he is unsure of what this is. He pauses briefly and then asks curiously "And?"

"They hated it. There was no enthusiasm at all. When I argued that it was only a first step and could be modified to match actual needs, one of the directors responded by describing the proposal as 'One giant leap into the unknown'."

Franck nods gravely. "Why do you think that they reacted the way that they did?"

"I think that they were a bit frightened by the proposal; it took us into an area where they had no experience or competence. How could they lead or manage if they hadn't a clue what we were changing? I also think that they were nervous because traditionally, as I said earlier, the sales process has been one of the key sensitive areas."

He nods.

"Well I panicked, and for the rest of the presentation I concentrated on the changes we were making which were primarily modifications to the existing processes. Towards the end of the meeting, out of the blue, one of the other directors asked for me to talk him through the overall process mapping again. I did and he suggested that it would be a good idea if each of the executives was responsible for one or more of the processes. A sort of high level sponsor or process owner. It seemed a good idea, I thought, and they all seemed very keen on the idea so that's what we did."

"What happened after the meeting?"

"Well after that we spent the bulk of our efforts improving the existing processes. We'd done a great job in mapping them so it was quite obvious where the holes were. We could show quick wins. Also the process owners seemed keen on localised improvements, they did not really encourage us to make changes which crossed too many functional boundaries."

"So you were tinkering with and tidying up the process?"

"Yes but we were getting some good results in efficiencies and opportunities to save costs."

"Save costs? I thought you were trying to re-engineer?"

"Well yes," I say hesitantly, "But you see we'd spent so much money we had to quickly find a way to get some of it back. How else could we have got the money back?"

"By increasing revenues?" he suggests in a smooth rolling tone of voice.

"But how could we? We didn't know how to use a process to increase revenue. We had only been mapping them, remember?"

"Why didn't you know how to use a process to increase revenue?"

Franck's question makes me pause. I'm stumped. I think silently, 'Why don't we know how to use the processes to increase revenue?' I look up at the ceiling, as if hoping the answer has been scribbled up there for me. Nothing. Another short moment passes. Franck remains both silent and very very still. And then it comes to me. 'We were so obsessed with how we did things internally, we never actually explored the customers' needs. We completely forgot what *the purpose of running the processes was, to produce something we could offer to customers* which would allow them *to part with their money* to us. We forgot it was about the *money making process.*' "Damn!" I exclaim. "Damn. Damn. Damn." I wedge my head between my hands.

"By **only** concentrating on cost reduction, I guess you missed a trick. To get the money you'd spent back you could either do it through reducing your operating costs, releasing or reducing the investment in the business or through increasing the revenues. Three choices, big trick."

"Yes sure, more than a trick though. Do you want to know what happened next?"

He nods vigorously.

"We were very successful in the internal process improvements we discovered. We remapped entire processes identifying opportunities for savings. Then we spent a small mountain of money building the IT application we needed to make the process run. Surprisingly and thankfully and I guess amazingly for an IT project, it went really smoothly."

I can tell from the expression on Franck's face that he hasn't come across the concept of an IT project which has gone smoothly. "Unfortunately the operating cost reductions identified were reductions in human input." I pause. "So to actually achieve the savings we had to initiate a redundancy program. It was terrible. I remember the day we announced the first group of redundancies. One of the junior staff came up to me and said, "First you ask us to help you to improve the business and then you use the improvements against us. I feel that you've made a fool out of me. I feel as if you've made this turkey vote for Christmas. And sharpen the butcher's knife." I was completely gobsmacked. I didn't know what to say. I remember mumbling something incomprehensible about it not all being down to me and corporate imperatives."

"How did that make you feel?"

"Terrible. Absolutely terrible. I guess I also realised that we would never get the trust and support of our staff for any future improvements we might wish to make." I pause briefly as the forgotten emotions of that time quickly sweep over me. "And then of course when we announced the first list of names, people were described as having been re-engineered out of a job. I guess that was when I realised that we had succeeded in making re-engineering synonymous in most people's minds with being fired, made redundant."

"Tough break," says Franck quietly and sympathetically.

"But there was worse to come. A month after we started the redundancy program our customer satisfaction rating fell dramatically. It fell not just because our staff were demotivated, but for a far more fundamental reason. The customers were complaining about the actual offer we were making them". I stare Franck straight in the face. "Do you understand what I'm saying? We'd *re-engineered in a process which had quickly passed its sell-by date.*" I continue in self reflection, "I guess it was partly because of what we discussed earlier, the fact that we hadn't looked at the customer's needs. But I guess it was also because the overall process we had implemented was very large, interlinked and rigid. The only way we could recover would be to rebuild the whole process and IT application again," I end disconsolately, "so here we are, two and a half million down, looking at other initiatives such as Business renewal, to move us forward because the business is still at risk."

<This time, the way I'll illustrate the movement back to the present, will be to describe a clock. The clock is circular with a white face, black hands and a gold rim. It hangs against a white wall about six feet up. Its diameter is roughly ten inches, which means that the time can be read quite easily from up to thirty feet. This time the camera focuses in tight on the clock face. Quietly but with grim determination the hands of the clock start to spin faster. Faster and faster and faster, now they are whizzing past. In no time at all, well, only a little, it's the present.>

Franck glances at his watch. A swift frown forms and dissolves on his forehead. He is obviously concerned that sharing stories is taking longer than he had anticipated. He tries to speed the process up. "I guess we can move onto the next participant. Don't take any notice of me."

A volunteer offers to be the next storyteller.

"Great. Please start. I am listening," he says as he stands to scribble on the whiteboard.

- *only learn what others don't already know*
- *focus*
- *delight and challenge*

The Twelf Tale
THE BUSINESS BENCH-MARKER'S TALE

I guess now I think of it, it wasn't very surprising. Top of the league in a sinking industry. It was as if we'd been judged the best but the best of what? The 'Queen of the pigs', that was us."

"Come on," he says encouragingly, "it can't be that bad."

"But it is. You see when we started to benchmark ourselves it made sense. We wanted to be able to guage ourselves against what the competition were up to. We hoped that by studying our competitors we would be able to work out more effectively where to target our energy."

"Sounds like a great idea."

"In theory, yes, but in practice no. The problem with benchmarking was getting the data. You see our competitors weren't just about to hand it over to us on a plate. That was the problem. The theory was fine but how did you actually get your hands on any meaningful data?" Franck shrugs.

"And then there was a stroke of luck. A major market research organization began to research the industry. It seemed that they had managed to set some yardsticks for performance. We bought a copy of their first report. The data looked fine, but we hadn't contributed to it so it was not a complete overview of the industry. The figures had estimated our sales, customer satisfaction and profitability and had got them wrong. They had also underestimated our in-pipeline contracts. Then we heard that some analysts were planning to use the report as a basis of their recommendations. Panic set in. We called the company, offering to provide our data and requesting to be re-entered."

"What happened next?"

"Well, in the next edition they included our data, but they must have underestimated or miscalculated their figures for all the other major players, because all the figures had changed significantly. I later found out that this was a common trick they use to get companies to provide what would otherwise be confidential information. Not very ethical."

"And?"

"We'd all been conned into providing a lot more information than we would otherwise have volunteered. In no time the publication became a bible for all the industry. We used it to set prices and raw materials costs. We now had the benchmark we'd been looking for."

"So what's the problem?"

"So we spent so long watching each other, so long tracking each other's every move we forgot to watch the customers and we forgot to look out for non-traditional competitors."

"I can see that could be a problem."

"But worse, we were paying a fortune for the reports, collection of benchmarking information and all the associated data. And, simply matching what the competitors were offering we were pushing up costs, but it was not having any upward effect at all on our actual sales. Our profitability was dropping like a stone."

"Sounds to me like you grew the problem yourselves."

"Thanks for the 20/20 hindsight," I say, sourly. "It all made sense at the time, what could we have done differently?"

"What do you think?"

"I don't know. That's why I'm talking to you."

"Why did you want the benchmarking information in the first place?"

I think only for a second and reply, "So that we could work out what to do next, where to focus our resources."

"So you wanted information to help you with the **future**?"

"I guess so," I reply non-committaly.

"And what did the publication give you?"

I don't know. "Facts?"

"Information about what competitors had already done. You wanted *predictive behaviour* and all you got from the publication was a *history lesson*. Perhaps you need to rethink the information you need and work out a way to get it. Fixating on the past is not the easiest way to create a bright future," advises Franck.

< as the present re-emerges it catches Franck writing three bullets.>

- *and!*
- *re-invent information*
- *show me the money*

Epilogue

That was fascinating," says the Strategic Change Implementer. "When you are struggling through these problems it's very lonely. You always feel as if you're the only one being put through the mill."

"Yeah," replies the Empowering Manager. "It's amazing how similar some of the issues were. I guess Franck would say that was the effect of the New World."

They are standing around a circular table heavily laden with food. Now they are having coffee, decaffeinated, since it is so late.

Franck announces, "Well I'm off. I'm a bit old to be up all night," he jokes. "See you in the morning. And thanks for being so open with us all."

3

Playing by the New Rules

Morning After Epilogue

'Science' simply means the aggregate of all the recipes that are always successful. All the rest is literature.

Paul Valery

The room that they occupy today is larger than the downstairs room they shared their tales in. Like the previous room, this one too is reminiscent of Zebra, its black beams and white walls providing the only decoration. The main difference is that the ceiling, this time, extends upwards, thirty feet upwards, like a barn. The room is north facing but light. Light because of the two large bay windows which practically fill the north wall.

Surprisingly the chairs and tables are arranged in a conventional half circle. Four flip chart stands, complete with thick pads of thin paper, stand to attention in each corner of the room. At the open end of the half circle is an overhead projector, its cross-wires trained on a square white screen.

Unsurprisingly the chairs are not conventional. With the room empty their curved backs, like a dozen green tricorn hats, or perhaps more like a dozen cocked hats, peeping above the tops of the wooden tables.

Now the twelve participants sit round in the half circle, expressions ranging from anticipation to impatience, worn on surprisingly wide awake faces. Surprising because it is seven o'clock in the morning.

"Thanks for getting here on time. I always feel it's worth an early start. If you're happy I'll make a start." With that, Franck turns on the projector and places his first slide on it. It is a re-written copy of the list from the electronic white board, still hand written. "I've taken the liberty of rewriting our list from last night," he says, "any objections?"

"I've rearranged and added to my previous thoughts on the Rules for the New World. I'm going to suggest we have dialogue, but I know that I'm so excited about all our discoveries that I'll probably end up making it a monologue. And I'll probably end up talking too fast. But please help me by asking questions. Let's all try and get as much out of this as possible. Is that a deal?"

Heads nod.

"Is that a deal?" he repeats. This time he is met by a chorus of 'Yeses' and 'okays'.

"Great. But before we start, I need to make a couple of points. Sometimes, although I've never said so, I find that people make two assumptions about what I say about the New World. The first is that it will be a Nirvana for us all. I don't believe that. In fact, I know that New World is very tough on many people. The second is that somehow human nature will be transformed and everyone will do the right thing. I don't believe that either. I do think that the aspects of culture which are cultural rather than human nature, will change in a New World environment. I believe that human beings will continue to be capable of the greatest good and the greatest evil and all the scales in between in their usual contradictory way. We will still want to be first and at the same time want our dearest ones also to be first, and our enemies to be last.

I simply assume that, in time, let me rephrase that, *it has already become too expensive, for some organizations, to be able to afford for many, if not most, of their highest paid and able people to spend significant amounts of time and effort on internal politics, power games, and personal foibles.* My guess is in time New World Organizations will increasingly banish such behavior and those particularly interested in such behavior. Those who thrive on the cut and thrust of internal politics will increasingly have to find it elsewhere. Those who come alive only because they can demonstrate and use their powerful positions, will find their hobby too expensive for most New World organizations to fund. They will have to look for opportunities to dominate their own personal suppliers. They will look forward to a trip to the supermarket, not as an opportunity to replenish supplies but instead as an opportunity to demonstrate the power of the customer. They will go on the internet." He grins. Franck obviously thinks that this is very funny. "The New Rules, I hope, *are your first step towards being first.*" He pauses to punctuate the moment. "Let's have a look at this list then."

New Rules for the New World

1   Say 'AND!' not 'OR'
    Paradox busting
2   Assume FAIR = DIFFERENT not FAIR = EQUAL
    Develop more styles
    Learn to communicate Purpose
3   Change DEPENDENCE to INTERDEPENDENCE
    Split Accountability from Responsibility
    Bet on teams AND networks AND the individual
4   Do NOTHING which is of NO use
    Show me the money!
    Focus!
    DO IT ONCE
5   Stakeholders rule OK!
    Know your stakeholders
    Trust first, then Tit-for-Tat
    Some suppliers more important than some customers
    Delight and Challenge the people you work with
6   Make time fit!
    Make TIME = PARALLEL
    Everything has sell-by dates
    Do it Now!
    Back from the Future
7   CHUNK IT OR JUNK IT!
    Modularize!
    Make it self similar
    Review too often!
8   ALL CONSTRAINTS INTO MEAT SPACE
    Re-invent your information
    Stay DIGITAL in Cyberspace
    Stop communicating!
9   Unlearn EVERYTHING!
    Every group a culture
    Only learn what others don't know!
10 Don't change anything!
    Beware the LAWS OF CHANGE
    Proact and React
    Seize the Future, Now!
    Respond with Awesome Velocity
    Robust or Bust!
11 LOOP IT UP!
    Form loops
    Break loops
12 Go VIRTUAL!
    Copy everyone imitate no-one
    Don't eat the menu!

Now they focus on the projector screen. Franck hands out photo-copies of the handwritten list. He pauses momentarily as he hands out each sheet of paper like a ham actor playing the part of someone doing something both momentous and historic. He is obviously aware of what he's doing. As he hands out the final copy to the Informatized manager who is now perched, expectant, at the head of the horseshoe arrangement, Franck grins broadly in self mockery and shrugs his shoulders. "I'd like you to read it through and see if you can spot the rules that tripped you up. I'm only suggesting that so you won't notice that I've misplaced my first slide and to give myself some time to find it." He rumages through the pile of transparencies. "Ah, here it is." He places a slide on the overhead projector. It has only one word on it. It says '*And*!'

Rule the Firste
SAY 'AND!' NOT 'OR'

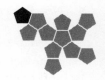

Frustration is the mother of risk

Gail Sheehy

"Children love '*And*!'. Can I have the chocolate cake with my dinner? Parents love 'Or'. Why? I believe that the very simple reason is that, '*And*!' can be terribly wasteful, '*And*!' can lead to food left on the plate. '*And*!' can lead to leftover dinner **and** sometimes left over chocolate cake."

"In an environment of stability, an environment where you can forecast the next few weeks or months relatively accurately, in an environment where most if not all customers are satisfied with the same things, in an environment where you **can** learn faster than the world changes, you would have to be dumb not to try to be as efficient as possible. Efficiency means better profits. Choosing to do **one thing** over **another** eliminates redundancy, forces repeats and increases efficiency. Perhaps that is why the Old World valued the consistent use of '**Or**'."

"Recently I was working with a group of managers discussing IT strategy. The organization had decided to move from Windows 3.11 to Windows 95. It had steam rollered the change across the whole organization, leaving behind a trail of disruption and despondency. The discussion was heated. Some of the executives who had been responsible for the decision were in the session. First there was discussion about the merits of 3.11 then discussion about the merits of 95. Then one executive commented, 'With these programs now branded by year, does that mean we have to throw everything away each year and start again?' The debate was loud and furious. Finally, I managed to get a word in. I asked, 'Tell me, how could we have applied an *And*?' There was silence, first they looked at me as if I was mad then they got the point. Then raucous laughter. You see there is no law which says you can't have both on the same machine. This could actually suit some users. Then one executive said, 'But that would cost a fortune. Kitting **everyone** out with both, doubling the license fee'. I replied then, that perhaps only using **one** New World rule was why he thought there was a problem. But now, I'm going to refer you to the second New World rule: *'fair = different'*. That rule will expose the Old World flaw in the executive's thinking. For now we need to carry on discussing *'And!'*

'And!' is most useful for paradox busting. It is also useful for **reducing risk** in a turbulent environment."

Paradox Busting

"The New World turns things on its head. In doing so it creates mental puzzles for us. Puzzles which appear insoluble, paradoxes. Or to be more accurate, paralyzing New World paradoxes.

Last year working in collaboration with one of my clients I worked on one of the few public/open events I have done in recent years. It was an evening of open discussion. We called it 'Overcoming the New World Paradoxes'. I have been actively collecting New World paradoxes for the past four years and working out ways to break the paradoxes. I have kept quite quiet about my work on paradoxes, largely because in the early Nineties it was very trendy in management circles to write books and articles with the word paradox in the title. I was afraid that my work would simply be lumped in with that great body of management material. And yet there is a Real World problem. A good paradox appears internally self consistent. It offers two distinct choices, each choice mutually exclusive of the other. I'll give you an example. It's my favorite one:

> *To make any money now and in the future we would have to concentrate on doing even better what we already do well today. This would mean that we would have to concentrate all our best people and key resources on improving the service offering we currently provide. At the same time, in order to make money both now and in the future we would have to find ways of doing things significantly differently. In order to achieve this we would have to focus the efforts of all our best people and resources on creating solutions for the future.*

All these words can be replaced by the simple diagram below:

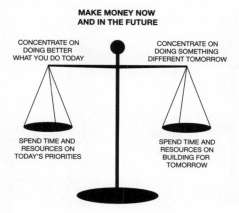

No! Don't go for a compromise. Tell me, are not *our* **key priorities** *the few things which we can* **benefit** *from now And!* *yet they provide a bridge or* *platform* *to the* *future?*

We must almost over prioritize such actions and studiously ignore, unless compelled not to, things which will **not** help us now or in the future, paying a little more attention to the things which help us **either** now **or** in the future. Future proofing, making our actions more resistant to the future and what it brings can be delivered effectively through *'And!'*. *'And!'* is a very effective paradox buster. Although there are other ways of busting paradoxes."

"Isn't it a bit wasteful to do things which may be completely redundant?" asks the Business Benchmarker in a voice which betrays that his question is actually a statement. He has already made his mind up.

"Of course it's wasteful," replies Franck. "What would you rather have in a New World environment, the efficient delivery of a product which no one buys because it is obsolete, or two wasted prototypes and reasonable sales?"

The Benchmarker nods.

"The paradox exists because there appears to be no overlap between the two choices. *'And!'* helps you find where two courses of action overlap. Does that make sense?"

The Benchmarker nods vigorously.

"Do you recognize any of these others from the tales? Do you have them in your organization? How could you bust them?" He draws on the flip chart:

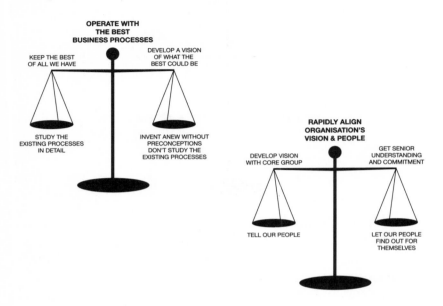

"Did you recognize any? Could you bust them? It is often worth listening out for other paradoxes your organization faces. *Often, the way to business success involves clearly describing the paradox, perhaps using my model of balanced scales, and then busting them.*

Each *paradox has the ability to* both *paralyze* the organization *or to over emphasize one train of thought or group of actions*. Remember, being paralyzed in the New World brings real risks. The rapid pace of change means that a month of indecision is an Old World year of dithering. As you wait, paralyzed, many things fill the time. Each a surprise. Surprising people with change is not the best way to get wholehearted support and buy-in. Each surprise brings with it a set of issues we weren't expecting. The continuous change is perceived as a threat to our security which in turn creates an emotional response from us, usually fear. The turbulence raises the emotional temperature since surprises lurk round every corner. *The only way to survive it is to **work in a New World way AND! have fun**.* Fun is the best antidote to emotional pressures.

"OK, well I can smell bacon, so I guess breakfast must be here. Should we eat?"

The participants rise to their feet and start athletically towards the doors. "Oh just one thing," he has to shout above the hubbub, "Please don't turn into one of those annoying people, drongos, who simply replace the word 'but' in a sentence with the word 'and' and then go on to pursue their **own** point **only**!"

Rule the Seconde
ASSUME FAIR = DIFFERENT

It were not best that we should all think alike; it is a difference of opinion that makes horse-races.

Mark Twain

"Perhaps it's even more deeply ingrained in us than we think. Perhaps it's something you believe as a kid and many of us have never grown out of. Did you have a brother or sister? Do you remember having to share? Do you remember how your parents told you that it was important to break biscuits, cakes, or indeed collections of dolls or marbles exactly into half. To be fair. To make sharing fair you would split the item(s) under dispute straight down the middle. **Fair = Equal**. Makes sense doesn't it?"

He places a transparency on the overhead projector.

FAIR = EQUAL

"In straight Old World business terms, Fair = Equal was a good maxim for operating. That made it a good assumption for thinking and as a result, was a great habit to have. But what do we now know? Now it is common for different customers to make different demands on us. In the Old World we were content to travel, with our customer groups along the product life cycle. We would happily work our way from early adopters through the majority, to the laggards feeling quite smug as each group of people acknowledged our product or service over a number of years. Different groups of people but the same product.

And now? In the New World, what happens for a start, is that a year, a year which used to be a **short** period of time, the measurement and review cycle, has now become a very **long** time indeed as more and more events are packed in. What product or service will survive successfully unaltered over the years it takes to travel down a product life cycle?

You find instead, that variations on the same product/service offer are being made simultaneously to all our customer groups. Indeed it is often more useful to break the customer groups in some other way than their speed and willingness to give us their money. It makes sense to break up our overall group of customers by what they need and want. And since they all seem to need and want something different, and the New World environment educates them in what they could need at the speed of light, they make their minds up and they don't all make their minds up the same way.

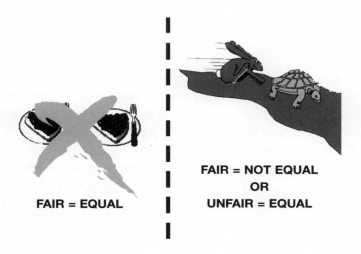

FAIR = EQUAL

FAIR = NOT EQUAL
OR
UNFAIR = EQUAL

A few years ago I was asked by an international banking operation to help them think through how to make more money out of an area of business which was coming under increased price pressure. The transfer of funds was managed and sold as a product called Drafts. A Draft could literally be for any amount from a couple of dollars to several tens of thousands. Both customers and the regulatory authorities were putting pressure on them to reduce the prices charged for the transfer of a Draft. What could be done?

I decided to attempt to apply *'Fair = Different'*. Any ideas on how this rule could be applied?"

There is a stunned silence.

"Come on. I'm sure you already know the answer, you just need to say it out loud to remind yourself that you do!"

"I guess you could look for areas where you are doing the same thing to a very large group of people?" suggests the Customer-Focused Manager, his voice trailing off at the end of the sentence.

"Precisely!" agrees Franck enthusiastically. "I told you you already knew the answer. The *first thing you do is look for areas of uniformity*. For example, was there a fixed percentage charged on all draft transfers? Were all drafts given the same priority? Do we have a single form/method for recording all customer requests?

It didn't take us long to find out that the answer to the questions above was, yes. Yes, and there were other things kept uniform, for example pricing was not dependent on customers. So guess what we did next?"

"Made those things different?"

"Eventually, but before we did that the *second thing we did was to look for areas of difference*. We did a quick customer need analysis on the overall group of customers served. Because we were interested in finding areas of difference we didn't do the usual thing of trying to discover what customers thought we did well or badly (which seems to be the focus of most market research). Instead, we concentrated on the areas where the information was harder to interpret. We looked for topics or products where customers seemed to be looking for different things. It rapidly became apparent that whilst some customers were extremely concerned about the price they were paying for each transfer, other customers were most concerned about speed and were critically interested in receiving information that a particular transfer had reached the other end. There were also some very strong emotions about the ease with which arrangements for a transfer could be made. He sketches out two axes, labels them with the demands he had said the customers were interested in and then marks four sided shapes on them.

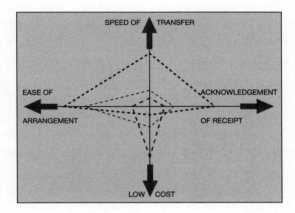

"This diagram shows the three most common patterns of difference. So what do we do now?"

The Empowering Manager volunteers, "Work out how we can be fair to each group separately and to ourselves as well?"

"Yep. And I guess it doesn't take a genius to work out what we should do next. Any suggestions?"

The participants have to respond. Not responding would signal that they were definitely **not** geniuses, a fact that most of us know to be true but don't necessarily admit in public. Finally, the Global Communicator makes a suggestion which is countered by the Empowering Manager. The discussion is vigorous. It ends with a coffee break.

Develop More Styles

"When the Strategic Implementer told us his tale it was very obvious that Change, with a capital C, has altered in nature. First it became apparent that *to achieve the goal* may require *different approaches* to the various *'chunks' of activity* s/he had to handle." Franck reads aloud notes he made the evening before.

I know that I'm stuck. You see, in order to *match the pace of change* and diversity of change of our customers and competition, it seems that we must *deliver* quickly tangible clearly *controlled and directed change.* This means that we *must encourage the implementation of closed projects,* change initiatives in which we **know what** to do and **how** to do it. On the other hand, in order to *match the pace and diversity of change forced upon us by our customers and competition,* we must explore widely delivering improvements which may only become attractive as we observe them. We must be able *to stick with intangible emergent deliverables.* That infers that we *must encourage open projects.* Changes where we either **do not** completely **know what** to do or **how** to do it.

And then, as we listened to the tale, we slowly began to realize that the changes to be implemented are different. And then slowly, for me, the realization dawned, that perhaps different styles of leadership were required. Another few minutes of description and now, of course, it's obvious. Different styles of leadership for different types of 'chunks'. In order to be fair to the situation and the people being led, you will need to demonstrate different behaviors. The New World demands *that to be continuously successful you put some energy into developing a range of styles to match the range of situations you face."*

He walks quickly across the room to the table below the bay window, retrieves a sheaf of papers and proceeds to hand them out. Each handout consists of four sheets stapled together. They say:

Type of Change	The Leader must be able to:

Closed:
Painting by Numbers
Know both WHAT to do
(goals are familiar) and
HOW to do it (methods
and technology are
familiar).

Demonstrate experience
Know and understand the methods and techniques employed in
the project
Clearly define goals
Clearly communicate the goals to all the groups of specialists
involved in the project
Set challenging standards
Assign tasks to team members
Define the boundaries between the tasks
Resolve conflicts and boundary issues
Be firm but fair in dealing with team members
Demonstrate a track record
Organize their own time
Plan activities for the whole project
Separate the essential many tasks from the critical few
Select the key skills and the behaviors required of the project
Identify corrective actions if the progress starts to deviate from
the plan
Offer motivation through reward and punishment
Reward and punish performance
Mange handover of deliverables
Prevent stakeholders external to the project from directly
influencing or modifying the tasks of the project team members
(unless a robust change management procedure is in place)

Other:
Find and negotiate with the project's stakeholders the
objectives of the project
Establish and record the hard success criteria of the project
Identify the soft criteria of the project
Establish contracts for delivery of the goal
Establish the critical chain of activities
Set milestones and points of delivery
Ensure that tasks are sequenced to maximize the productivity of
the resources (human and business)
Construct a reporting system which provides information on
project progress
Be able to track progress (financial and non-financial) against
the plan
Keep the output stakeholders informed and in balance
Understand how to make up (time or money) on the project

Type of Change	The Leader must be able to:
Semi-closed: **Going on a Quest** Know WHAT but don't know HOW.	Understand the nature of the problem faced

Encapsulate the solution to the problem in a persuasive manner

Develop a vision to accompany the solution

Communicate the vision enthusiastically and persuasively

Gain personal ownership for the idea from the team members

Select team members capable of pursuing the challenge

Live the values embodied in the project

Offer motivation through 'fame and fortune' opportunities to discover or fear of having let down the team or retribution of 'believers against unbelievers'

Must be single minded (almost to the point of obstinacy)

Be able to learn from stakeholders their success criteria and then to reinterpret their criteria in line with the overall vision in order to gain their interest and commitment

Keen and willing to try methods which the leader does not fully understand in order to achieve the goal

Avoid undue overlap and duplication of lines of enquiry

Assign tasks to team members

Set limits to each line of enquiry on the basis of time or resources (financial or non-financial) called checkpoints

Strictly and fairly enforce the limits to each line of enquiry

Monitor progress by the elimination of unfruitful lines of enquiry

Encourage sharing of learning across the team from each line of enquiry

Maintain the vision and its seductiveness in the light of short-term failure

Demonstrate courage

Show genuine concern for team members

Other:

Establish financial contracts which acknowledge the nature of the project (over-run clauses, etc.)

Gather team/information for reviews of each line of enquiry

Co-ordinate activity so that several routes (methods - how) are investigated simultaneously (subject to resource availability)

Manage stakeholders (especially those responsible for resources) to maintain access to key resources especially as the project begins to over-run

Establish and record the hard success criteria of the project

Identify the soft criteria of the project

Ensure that tasks are sequenced to maximize the productivity of the resources (human and business)

Construct a reporting system which provides information on project progress at each checkpoint

Be able to track progress (financial and non-financial) against each phase of the plan

Keep the output stakeholders informed and in balance

Type of Change	The Leader must be able to:
Semi-open: **Making a Movie** Know HOW Don't know WHAT.	Be persistent in defining the goals of the project Hold a steady vision in his/her head for long periods of time Be more interested in the goal of the project than in the use of the method or technology Be almost obsessive about high-quality standards Find opportunities for team members to use their skills to the fullest Set challenging personal visions for team members Demonstrate experience or understanding of the main technology or methodology used Build a vision of the project goals from stakeholder aspirations Be prepared to adjust or modify the initial goals as further objectives are identified Keep the use of the methodology as far in the background as possible without de-motivating the team Be able to speak the language of the team specialists Assign roles to team members Review progress against the vision Continuously review quality and not move on until the deliverables meet the quality objectives of the vision Be able to hold a wide range of activities in his/her head (alongside the vision) and co-ordinate them Be able to raise the visibility of the vision among the team Make sure that the team all understand how their role contributes to achieving it Prevent the team from delivering results not in line with the vision Provide space for creativity in line with the vision Demonstrate aspects of the vision Motivate through relationships Appear to know all the team personally **Other:** Establish appropriate contracts for the project Monitor resource use in line with the overall vision Find the project's stakeholders and sell the objectives of the project (called romancing) Modify the objectives until the goal is in line with business needs and is plausible Establish and record the hard success criteria of the project Identify the soft criteria of the project Establish contracts for the delivery of the methodology Establish the chain of activities Ensure that tasks are sequenced to maximize the productivity of the resources (human and business) Construct a reporting system which provides information on project progress Be able to track progress (financial and non-financial) against the plan Keep the output stakeholders informed and in balance Develop contingencies which might also meet the vision

Type of Change	The Leader must be able to:
Open: **Lost in the Fog** Don't know WHAT to do exactly or HOW to do it.	Build trust Make promises and keep them Find a wide range of stakeholders many of whom do not initially see themselves as stakeholders Be prepared to come to you (match and lead) Communicate widely and effectively Listen effectively to both logical and emotional concerns Demonstrate calmness (even when panicking) Describe and capture the nature of the problem faced Clearly articulate a vision (usually the opposite of the problem faced) Show genuine concern for the team Keep stakeholders informed on a day-to-day basis Encourage the team to communicate amongst themselves Capture any learning the team makes Proceed one step at a time Appear to know where s/he is going intuitively Reassure team members Be creative with any new opportunities or insights which present themselves Give hope to the stakeholders Praise initiative taken by the team Provide intellectual challenge through questioning and problem description Analyze complex situations and distill the few actions likely to give the biggest results Accept offers of ideas and efforts from the team Involve team in decision making Ensure ownership of each intermediate plan amongst team **Other:** Plan-Do-Review-Learn in short rapid cycles Establish appropriate contracts for the project (cost plus) Monitor resource involvement in line with solving overall problem Keep seeking out project's stakeholders Educating project stakeholders on new areas and project deliverables Establish and record the hard success criteria of the project Identify the soft criteria of the project Establish contracts for the delivery of the methodology Construct a reporting system which captures any learning made during the project's progress Be able to track progress (financial and non-financial) against size and desirability of solving the problem Keep the output stakeholders informed and in balance Maintain stakeholders' expectations in balance at all times

"Are there any questions?" Franck gives the group about a minute and a half to study the documents. "Any comments?"

"Here, where it says, painting by numbers, quest, fog and so on, what's that?"

"Just a bit of fun. I have nicknames for the different types of chunks of change. The nicknames are shorthands for similar situations."

The Strategist asks, "Does this apply to strategic change too?"

Franck replies, "*Strategic change is weird, strategic change is different, with strategic change you yourself may never experience the effect of the events you set in train*. There is even greater reason to make sure that the leader's behavior matches the type of change or else you may experience further unexpected and unwanted effects of emergence."

The Strategist nods in response.

"Should we move on?"

Learn to Communicate Purpose

"Usually a particular method or process leads to a restricted range of outputs. But, increasingly, in a New World environment, as technology converges and diverges[22], these days you can get to the same result in several different ways. I mean think about it, you want to keep a record of someone's phone number, do you, a. put it on the company database? b. write it in your filofax? c. put it on your electronic personal organizer? d. scribble it on a post-it? In most things, except software," he grins mischievously, "the choices are enormous. What does this have to do with the rule, '*fair = different*'?" he asks rhetorically. "I believe the trick is to *become more and more effective at communicating the intended outcome* and encouraging creativity for a range of different approaches."[23]

Rule the Thirde
CHANGE DEPENDENCE TO INTERDEPENDENCE!

> *When I was a boy my Father was wise. When I grew up I was amazed to discover how stupid he had become.*
>
> Mark Twain

"Money gives, as it always has, the illusion of independence even in situations of dependence. Unless of course you can fix your own car, re-roof your own house, mend all the roads you drive on and are a dab hand at brain surgery, you are dependent on others. And yet, with enough money the illusion of independence is complete.

Inside organizations, in the Old World, budgets fulfilled the same illusory function. Budgets set by function or department convinced everyone who used the codes that they were independent of others in the organization. They assumed, no, believed, that they could succeed independently of others in the organization. The budgeting process, however, re-enforced the conclusion of dependence. Dependence on the few people who controlled the budgets and without whom any individual's plans would be thwarted.

Net result, in the Old World, Budget time is a blood bath. People fighting within the dependence they have, for the highest levels of apparent independence, once the budgets are signed off.

I guess that there's nothing really wrong with the illusion. In a world which changes slowly and in a world where it is possible to learn faster than events change it, customer demands change slowly. A year is still a short time. As a result, misalignment of goals across departments or functions happens slowly. There is plenty of time to make adjustments to unbalanced resources through the annual planning and budgeting cycle. The approximation works. We treat areas of the business as dependent only during the planning cycle, align them and then for the rest of the time they are free to operate as independent. It provides clarity of responsibility and control. The problem only arises as the New World dawns. Then we discover that *we have more change than we can comfortably fit into our planning cycle.* We discover *that we need more alignment than we can command from the top. We need more leaders than we can find in the upper echelons of the organization.* Then, and only then, do we become tempted to reduce the level of dependence on the top of the organization. Then and only then, do we try to encourage others further flung across the organization to help with the tasks of leading change, aligning themselves and planning their own actions. Empowerment, the buzzword of the early nineties, looks attractive but..."

He turns to the Empowering Manager and asks, "What was it you said? You described the big problem you had with empowerment?"

For a second the Empowering Manager looks blank and then he replies, "Oh yes, *you tell people that they are empowered and they interpret that as: 'I can do what I want without telling anyone else'*".

As he speaks Franck is drawing furiously on the board.

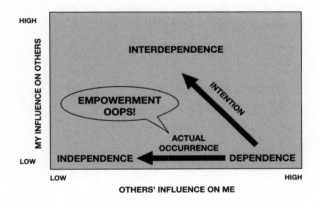

Franck responds, pointing to the diagram on the flip chart. "If you really want *to create interdependence you need to completely re-invent how you see the individuals, how you assign tasks and how you intertwine roles.* You need to reinvent how tasks are assigned." As he speaks he writes bullet points on the flipchart.

- Assign each task to more than one person, perhaps a lead and support –
  "rewards are offered".
- Plan reward structures which only kick in if contributions of more than one person are included –
  "you plan group tasks".

- Planning sessions should focus on the links between the activities different people are pursuing –
  "you organize accountabilities".
- Create joint accountabilities, often clearly defining if there is a chain of accountabilities –
  "information is collected and shared".
- Provide shared repositories for information. Also make one person highly dependent on the information provided by another.

"How about five minutes, in buzz groups, to discuss how what I've just suggested affects you as a New World manager?"

Split Accountability from responsibility

"Have you come across the Old World symbol which looks like this?" He draws a symbol on the flip chart.

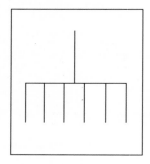

"I'm sure you have. It's an amazing symbol. In the Old World it transcended industry sectors, company size, geography and everything else. There were few organizations that it had not infiltrated and taken over. A symbol so potent it could determine how much you were paid, how many ceiling tiles your office had and the number of cc's in your corporate limo. It was omnipresent and pretty potent. Indeed, I came across many managers who would insist that the symbol and all it represents had existed forever. They believed that it was a symbol, which indeed, had existed before time. Was borne of the natural order and human nature. A magical and religious icon, never to be trifled with."

The group laughs.

"But what did it mean? I'm reliably told by people who know about that sort of historical information, that it represented something called the reporting line, something to do with a command and control hierarchy?"

His pitch rises at the end of the sentence making it a question and at the same time introducing a hint of mockery. There is more laughter but this time it is less universal.

"What do you think are the main assumptions underpinning the choice to operate in a command and control hierarchy?"

"I guess *the person in command needs to get it right,*" says the Chief Executive.

"Any others?"

"That *the person who demands the work is a customer for the work,*" offers the Customer-Focused Manager,

"That *it is possible for someone to tie all the strands together effectively to achieve the intended output.*"

Franck interjects, "This usually means that *the processes are well defined and preferably repeated* often. Great. Any others..."

"That *the person in command CAN get it right.* I mean has the experience of similar situations," interjects the Informatized Manager who has been sitting quietly for a while.

"Yes I agree," replies Franck nodding furiously, "Any of you have businesses where these prerequisites are present? Are present all the time? Are present all the time in all your activities?"

The room is silent.

"OK, in the Old World the lines of reporting were such that the person who was *count*ed on to deliver (accountable)," he says, almost as an aside to a hidden camera, "was the same as the person who was expected to have the *capability* to *respond* (responsible). In the New World environment because the pre-requisites often don't apply it often makes sense to split the accountability from the responsibility. What you want is *for individuals or teams to say, 'You can count on me to deliver'.* And you want them to say this to the stakeholders who will be the customers of the project or process activity they are performing. At the same time, you want to make sure that there are people in the organization who have the *capability to respond* to requests. These people will be responsible for groups of your people. *They will make* *sure that the people whom they are responsible for have the capabilities, skills, rewards and motivations which allow them to be able to promise to deliver.* In early days it was most common to observe this sort of split in project based organizations, like contractors. Nowadays it is increasingly common to find yourself doing a piece of work for someone who isn't your 'boss'."

On a flip chart he draws:

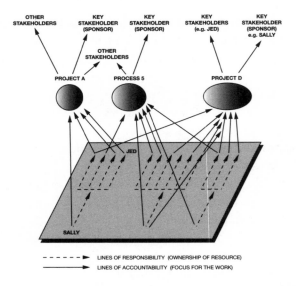

"This," he says, "is the reality of the situation most people find themselves in, in the real world. But," he stresses, "people keep describing this reality using the old comb shape. So what happens? We find ourselves re-organizing and re-organizing in order to try to get our activities to fit the two dimensional linear organizational pyramid. Although the reality of the situation can only be represented by three or more dimensions. Guess what happens with our re-organizations? All that happens is that some parts fit better whilst others fit worse, forcing us into yet another re-organization."

There is silence. A deep silence. The sort of deep silence that usually follows an inappropriate or embarrassing comment. Then the Organization Development Manager clears his throat and says, "Now I'm completely depressed. It is all so obvious if you apply common sense."

"I know," says Frank smugly, "should we carry on?"

Bet on Teams AND Networks AND the Individual

"Old World 'Or' thinking seems to predominate in this area. Organizations are swinging from operating though individuals to operating in teams. At the same time individual performance, pay-for-performance and individual assessment and appraisal are being encouraged. In larger organizations people are encouraged to network amongst themselves. In smaller organizations they are being encouraged to network with others outside the organization, through associations, through common issue groups.

Companies are drawing battle lines, putting their bets on teams, self-directed, self-managed or virtual. Where the team reigns, the individual is silenced, well except in those long tortuous rambling early team meetings."

The Self-Directed Team leader protests, "Stop picking on me".

Frank raises his eyes to the ceiling and wobbles his head about with a smile on his lips, "I wasn't really thinking about anyone in particular. Anyway, I believe that the trick is *to encourage the people in the organization into the right configuration, a **configuration best suited for** what they are trying to **achieve** at that point in time, and a configuration which allows them to be happy and flourish and **brings out the best** in them.*"

Franck draws four columns on the flip chart. He suggests, "Why don't we brainstorm common situations or challenges which require effective action." Five minutes later a list has been produced including situations such as 'Improving existing processes'. Now he suggests, "Why don't we try to rank the effectiveness of individuals, teams or networks in each of the situations?" Half an hour passes and the flip-chart ends up like this:

	Individual	Team	Network
Improving existing processes and thinking	✔ ✔ Some individuals far exceed entire teams in their creativity	✔ ✔ ✔	✔ Networks often do not share processes
Innovating outside the organization's 'recipe'	✔ ✔ ✔	✔ ✔	✔ Networks are rarely cohesive enough to make an impact
Bringing a wide range of skills to bear on a problem	✔	✔ ✔ ✔	✔ ✔ ✔
Learning by integrating a range of inputs	✔ ✔ Some individuals are very eclectic	✔ ✔	✔ ✔ ✔
Providing continuity	✔ ✔	✔ ✔ ✔	✔
Maintaining excellence	✔ ✔ ✔	✔ ✔ ✔	✔
Meeting objectives	✔ ✔	✔ ✔	✔
Exploring new opportunities	✔ ✔	✔	✔ ✔ ✔
Responding to competition	✔ ✔ ✔	✔ ✔ ✔	✔ Networks often do not share common goals
Carrying out clearly specified repetitive tasks	✔ ✔ ✔	✔ ✔	✔
Providing specialist focus	✔ ✔ ✔	✔ ✔	✔
Being a heretic	✔ ✔ Some individuals excel at this	✔ ✔	✔ Networks are rarely cohesive enough to make an impact
Spotting opportunities	✔ ✔	✔ Teams often focus on shared and common goals not actively seeking new ones	✔ ✔
Providing emotional support	✔	✔ ✔ ✔	✔ Rate of change of membership affects this
Managing stakeholders	✔ ✔ ✔	✔ ✔	✔ Lack of clear accountability makes this difficult
Focusing on customer needs	✔ ✔	✔ ✔	✔ Lack of clear accountability makes this difficult
Policing its own activities	✔ Many individuals judge themselves by their intentions rather than their actions	✔ ✔ Low motivation teams sometimes collude in poor performance	✔ Lack of clear accountability makes this difficult
Providing intellectual challenge	✔ ✔ ✔	✔ Teams made up of different specialisms find it it difficult to challenge each other at the leading edge	✔ ✔ ✔

There is only one real discussion as the chart is produced. The Strategist starts to argue with the Self-Directed Team Leader over the definitions of *common goals* and *the role of interdependence*. The rest of the group listen to the arguments for a while and then Franck interjects, "Don't forget," he says sternly, almost as if he wants to punctuate his next statement, "*that you can be interdependent without having common goals.*" With that he draws a diagram on the other flip chart:

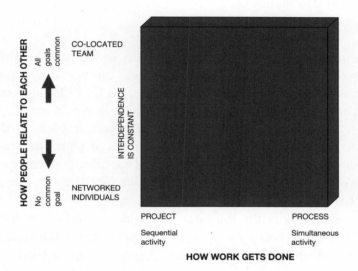

"Think," he instructs, "about the Internet. It is pointless having a net server with a website without the existence of the rest of the Internet. You depend on them and they depend on you. And yet there may not be any common goals shared at all!"

Speaking thoughtfully, the Self-Directed Team Leader adds, "I see what you're saying."

"Perhaps," he suggests, and then speaking in distinct syllables, as if trying to over-emphasize the point he says, "*To win, you bet on teams, networks AND the individual. You must master leadership and followership and networking and know when to do which, you must master reaching out TO help and reaching out FOR help and you must master yourself.*" He stands square to the group, the corners of his mouth turned downward as if to say, 'This is the message.', grins suddenly and asks, "Should we have a short break for some coffee?"

The Forthe Rule
DO NOTHING WHICH IS OF
NO USE!

If work were a good thing, the rich would have found a way of keeping it to themselves.

Haitian proverb

"What an Impossible Demand. In a world which has the ability to change far faster than you can learn, surely this is asking too much. But surely, it's the other way round. In such a bewilderingly complicated and chaotic world *it becomes impossible to handle an increasing number, no, infinite challenges, opportunities and problems with what can ever only be finite resources, your time and your organization's resources*. Can you see? More and more of the things which affect you are out of your control. It becomes critical to focus on changes which help, changes which are improvements."

He walks over to the the large bay window and stares out for a second. "You see, one of the things we forget is that in the more stable Old World business environment, any changes we got involved in had been looked at, studied, vetted and approved by other people more senior to us who might have better answers and at least had more relevant experience than we had. As a result anything passed to us to 'change' was probably not entirely a dog of an idea. *Most of the change we undertook had been understood as useful in the context of what we knew the organization needed*. The problem in the New World is that *it is essential to recognize that Change and Improvement are NOT the same thing*." He grabs a black marker pen and on the nearer of the flip charts, draws a large circle across which he writes the word "CHANGE". Then in red ink he draws a small circle, smaller than a small coin. "Can you see this?" he says pointing at the red circle.

His audience responds with uncertain nods and a loud comment of 'barely'.

"If the big circle here is Change, this," he says, moving his arm with a flourish as if to wipe over it, "this, is improvement."

"Change and Improvement are not the same thing," he restates. "What," he asks, "is the difference between change and improvement?"

There is no response. Franck waits.

"Good change?" offers the Self-Starter.

"Precisely! Change simply means alteration whereas Improvement is an alteration which brings your goals closer. So improvement is meaningless unless you have a view of what your goals are. For an individual, if you are like me, you would probably argue that the goal of life is Fun and Learning. Others would put a religious spin on it and say it was to serve God. All very subjective. *For business organizations, especially publicly owned ones, the goal is simple; to make money. For non-business organizations it is worth going back to the original charter* of the organization."

Franck pauses briefly waiting for comment or dissent. There is none. "Should I continue?" he asks. Gently nodding heads urge him onward.

"I guess the most important aspect of *'Do nothing which is of no use'* is not this aspect of change, the almost directional aspect, but the way of thinking it brings with it. You see, *'Do nothing...'* is a mind-set which should help you *focus only on change which is aimed at goals, or at eliminating threats to current achievements.* As we saw in the tale from the Empowering Manager, it is important to make sure that all the people in the organization have acquired this mind-set. But, in addition, there is another equally important aspect which is *the determination to use everything.* A project fails to deliver anticipated sales,

'Do nothing...' insists that you learn all you can from that failure, so that it can be applied effectively somewhere else. You start out on a visit to a customer, a thirty mile drive, halfway there your mobile rings and the customer announces that s/he is having to cancel the meeting. *'Do nothing...'* insists that you go through your organizer to see if there is anyone else in the vicinity you could visit instead. *'Do nothing...'* insists that you look to see if your meeting preparation notes apply to anyone else. Adapting to provide new outcomes is a key message of, *'Do nothing which is of no use'."*

Show Me the Money!

"For the simplest case, business organizations, there are four questions it is critical to ask, to check if a change is an improvement[24]."

1 *Will this change help us make money faster now or in the future?*[25]
2 *Will it reduce the rate at which we have to spend money to operate, now or in the future?*
3 *Will it release money tied up in the business?*
4 *Does it help us to meet (externally imposed) necessary conditions.*[26]

"I have found that any change which doesn't answer, 'Yes' to at least one of these questions, is probably **someone else's** irrelevant pet project." Franck stresses the words 'someone else's' and then grins a wide toothy grin.

Focus!

"*'Do nothing...'* also imposes pressures on focus. I tend to use constraints as the route to identifying areas of focus in complex problems. The question you are asking is, *'What few things are really stopping us achieving the goals we wish to attain?'* These few things are constraints. By focusing on the constraints we have a simple and easy route to reaching the goals."

Franck walks across to the table in the bay window, retrieves a pile of pink-colored A3 sized sheets and some A4 white handouts. "I use bubble diagrams[27]," he says. "There isn't enough time to practice but I'm giving you all you need. You will have to work it out in your own time.

BUILDING A BUBBLE DIAGRAM

Step 1 Get three sheets of A3 paper.

Step 2 On the first sheet write down (as sentences) the major business problems which concern you.

Step 3 Choose three or four which are suitably different or seem unrelated.

Step 4 Place your second sheet landscape and write out the problems, in bubbles starting about a third of the way down.

Step 5 Start with the problem you feel most confident that you understand. Guess a cause and check the effects. Keep checking until you are satisfied that your guess is either right or wrong. Draw an arrow from the cause to the effect or problem.

Step 6 Stay with the same bubble. Do not move into another one yet. Repeat Step 5 until you have run out of guesses for that single problem.

Step 7 Go to the next problem and repeat Steps 5 and 6. You may find that some of the guesses or effects you ahve written down are guesses or effects which you need as you work on this second problem. If you find that this is the case, don't duplicate what you have already written, simply join up the bubbles with arrows (IF ⇨ THEN or WHY? ⇦ BECAUSE).

Step 8 Repeat step 7 for the remaining one or two problems.

Step 9 Read what you have written down and see if you can add any more arrows. Try to link to the problems you started with. (If you need an 'AND', record this by a horizontal bar across two arrows).

Step 10 Check to see if you can trace, without lifting your pencil off the page, a line which goes up or down any arrows and passes through all the problems you started with. If you can, skip to step 12.

Step 11 Look for bubbles which don't have any arrows going to them. For each one of these bubbles, go back to Step 5.

STEP 12 Go back to your first sheet and read through your list of problems. You will see that on your bubble diagram you have written down their causes. Fill in the top third of your second sheet with bubbles of the remaining problems. (In the very unlikely event that you cannot directly transfer one or two of your list of problems directly onto the bubble chart, write them in the top third and go back to Step 5).

Step 13 You now need to fill in the top of the second sheet. For each of the original problems, complete the sentence IF {original problem} THEN ___ {new bubble to be drawn in above the original problem bubble}. Now your bubble chart should also have some of the problems you feel you have but did not include on your original list because you felt that they were less weighty!

Step 14 Look for the remaining bubbles which do not have an arrow going to them. Choose one and guess a cause, and check the effects. Keep checking until you are satisfied that your guess is either right or wrong. Stay with the same bubble; do not move onto another until you have run out of guesses for that single problem.

> Step 15 Repeat Step 14 until you come across bubbles which are
> **clearly out of your control and influence**:
> "the Government have just passed new legislation",
> "Competitors have just launched a new product",
> or the **cause is historic**:
> "we were taken over in 1978",
> or **the result of a policy**:
> "We pay people by the hour",
> "Our staff are paid a large bonus for production quantity",
> or it may be a **physical reality**, such as:
> "we just haven't got enough of the right type of staff",
> "our equipment cannot manufacture any faster".
>
> These bubbles will explain the underlying causes. It is unusual to have more than half a dozen, so if you have more you may be doing something wrong. Usually it is because you have tried to force the process to come up with your pet theory and your checks on effects have not been rigorous. Never mind: Step 16 should sort you out.
> Step 16 You are going to read the bubble chart back to yourself, out loud, to check that you haven't gone wrong anywhere. Start at the bottom and follow the arrows upwards.

"Please read through the instructions and let me answer any questions you have."

"How long does this take to do?" asks the Business Benchmarker.

"Simple problem, mmm, an hour, complex problem about three hours over a couple of days."

Do it Once

"'*Do nothing which is of no use*'" can also be interpreted in another way, I describe that as '*Do it once*'. '*Do it once*' is a way of thinking which covers the more conventional '*right first time*' concept. But more importantly it is a mind-set which encourages you to think *through* a problem and its implementation far into the future, to the end point, if there is one. So, '*Do it once*' makes sure that you check that the final output is what you actually want. Of all the New World rules, this is the only one which seems to have been violated consistently by all of you as your various tales say.

In practice a '*Do it once*' philosophy is behind a number of good rules of thumb. For example the New World practice of appealing to a wide range of segments by *providing a multi-offer*."

"What is a multi-offer?" asks the Customer-Focused Manager.

"Er," Franck searches his memory for an example. "Er, yes I know. Have you noticed with music, the increasing success and popularity of multi-offers, boy bands with a 'look' for each segment, girl bands with girls with five different looks and hair colorings, albums by one group with tracks with styles which range from rock and roll to reggae?"

"Yes."

"Multi-offer," he says, acting as if his example had actually been illuminating rather than just an interesting observation. "Each facet of the offer is aimed at a particular market segment. *One whole offer, offer targets many segments, multi-offer,*" he announces triumphantly.

"I can see how that works with music and perhaps even with services but what about products, manufactured goods?" quizzes the Chief Executive.

"Multi's are more difficult with manufactured goods. In the past they took the form of free giveaways, for example plastic toys in your box of cereal. Or a free spanner set with a new bicycle. A real multi is not a giveaway. *With a real multi you get what you want from an offer and so do others even though you might be after different things.*"

The other angle on *'Do it once'*, relates to the mind-set I described first. The trick often is to *position every offer within another offer*[28]. So you find that films are written with the merchandising opportunities already present in embryo."

The Fifthe Rule
STAKEHOLDERS RULE OK!

We shape our buildings. Thereafter they shape us.

Winston Churchill

"In the New World, *simple relationships* such as boss/subordinate are often *replaced by more complex ones*; project leader/specialist resource, functional head/internal consultant. Unless we change our ability to describe these relationships, the operation of the organization becomes complicated. A route is to think about **stakeholders**. So, who are these stakeholders? Well, it seems that anytime anything changes there are interested parties. Because there are two ways in which change happens: *sequential* (usually described as a project or program), *where one activity follows another* and as a result the people experiencing the change are involved in different things from day-to-day, and *simultaneous* (usually described as process) where *concurrent activities* acting on the same piece of information, material or human need, combine to create the change – here, although each person may be carrying out the same activities day-in-day-out, the inputs are transformed into something different.

Sequential change tends to upset stakeholders far more than simultaneous change. For this reason you will find that *process stakeholders are not always immediately obvious.*"

Know Your Stakeholders

"Stakeholders hold a stake because achieving the output or outcome of your process, project or program affects them.

To work out who the stakeholders are, you need to:

- Think about all the **people** who you need:
  — as resources
  — to take along
- Think about all the **people** who your process or project output or execution:

— is likely to affect directly or indirectly

- Think about all the **people** in the sidelines:
  — watching you and making judgments about what the project or process will be providing."

He writes the bullet points upon a flip chart as he speaks. "It is easiest to organize the names and groups as a **grid** or a **map**." He hands out another document.

STAKEHOLDER MAP

PROCESS OR PROJECT
Output/Outcome *(if known)*

Stakeholders

Who receives the output?

Who provides inputs (information, materials, people)?

What specialist skills are used?

Who provides capability?

Who is the constrained resource?

Who is responsible for the constrained resource?

Who decides the scheduling?

Who wants it to:
    succeed?
    fail?

Who is betting on it to:
    succeed?
    fail?

Who is supporting it:
    visibly?
    invisibly?

Whose success:
    affects you?
    do you affect?

Who does your change:
    benefit?
    damage?

Who can your change:
    happen without?
    not happen without?

Absolutely critical: _____ Outcome interest: o   Interest during: *

Trust First, and then Play Tit-for-Tat

"The biggest downside to working in several overlapping virtual teams is a **real** problem. You need to be sure that you are happy to be interdependent with all the people you interact with. But there is not enough time to go through the traditional reference and positive vetting process.

One of the best bits of work on co-operation and competition in nature, was carried out by a geezer called John Holland. He studied a number of complex strategies to determine which had the most impact for a player in an environment where s/he could face co-operation or competition[29]. They used computer programs to explore a wide range of potential strategies. By far, the winner was a very simple strategy, Tit-for-Tat.

They discovered that by starting each action in co-operative mode the Tit-for-Tat strategy incorporated the essence of carrot and stick. *It was* **nice** *in the sense that it would never be aggressive first. It was 'forgiving' in the sense that it would reward good behavior by* **co-operating** *the next time. And yet it was 'tough' in the sense that it would punish uncooperative behavior. Moreover it was 'clear' in the sense that its strategy was so simple that it was apparent to any other agent who could then respond appropriately.*

For the New World, I believe that making people aware that you operate Tit-for-Tat always, without fail, with a vengeance, can be very effective. *It encourages them to think twice about how their actions will affect you. It also allows you to win allies and extend your leadership rapidly amongst people who don't have any particular hidden agenda.*

There is nothing that new about Tit-for-Tat strategies. They have been played by several of the world's most successful entrepreneurs and capitalists for years (and have even been popularized in films like *The Godfather* about closed societies). Quite simply put, "If you play fair by me I'll play fair by you, but if you cross me..."

Easy to describe, Tit-for-Tat is harder to apply to some stakeholders than others; for example in strong hierarchies, significant creativity is required in order to be able to effectively apply it to people far more powerful than yourself."

Some Suppliers More Important than Some Customers

"As the New World unfolds it becomes increasingly obvious that good, Old World, linear relationships are over-simplistic. *Even popular philosophies, like 'customer focus' and 'the customer is king' which on first view look rational, look like common sense, are wrong!* The customer, our source of revenue **must** be key we think. But as you inspect the idea more closely, the common sense it appears to possess, starts to evaporate. Think about it. As we have less and less time to cram in all the things required for effective operation, into the time available, it becomes more and more difficult to find and source new suppliers. In many cases the savings gained by switching suppliers can easily be outweighed by the costs of switching and often there isn't actually the breathing space required. Also, as technologies converge and diverge, *betting on the right supplier to give you a competitive advantage becomes increasingly critical.* The first place that this New World application of the fifth rule was seen, was through arrangements like preferred supplier relationships and strategic alliances. Now, increasingly, in more and more organizations success is more and more obviously dependent on access to and support from some key suppliers. In their turn suppliers with less and less resource for chasing after new customers are asking themselves more frequently, 'Which customers are best strategically? Which customers are thriving and will continue to demand our input and also as importantly, which customers should we offer our latest innovations to first?'

Taken from both points of view you can see why I am dissatisfied with the old slogans. Think about it. It is obvious that whilst many customers are more important to overall success than suppliers, some suppliers are more important than some customers. I challenge you to extend that thinking into the organization. Into internal customer and supplier relationships." Finally Franck pauses.

"Do you have any examples of how this works?" quizzes the Business Benchmarker. "I mean how do you stop your suppliers ripping you off if you go soft on them?"

"A common example of this thinking, is the practice of *outsourcing* by *paying well* and then *demanding too much*. This forces the customer supplier relationship towards flexibility and towards delivering outputs focused on success. The supplier is constantly forced to innovate and produce improvements for what is their best customer. The customer gains competitive advantage from the star treatment."

He turns to a virgin chart and draws a diagram:

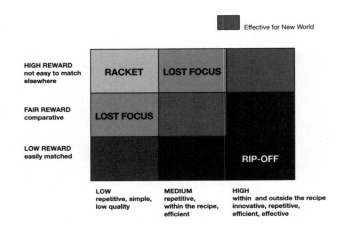

"I believe that unwittingly the thinking has been adopted by organizations during their downsizing/rightsizing activities of the past half decade. Most organizations have achieved the *demand too much* part of the idea, without the *pay well* bit. Those who have, have used other routes such as merger activities to achieve the result. Ideally, commitment through overpay and overdemand is long term. In practice, there is a risk of burn-out. I think it's worth spending some time, fifteen minutes, in buzz groups discussing the relative value to us of key suppliers vs. customers."

Delight and Challenge the People You Work With

"Let's face it. You like to work with people you like, or at least respect. *Stakeholders are people. Most people are human beings*. Human beings are a complex species, who, in the main, thrive on a complex cocktail of emotional, religious, logical, and instinctive behaviors. This makes it very hard to pin them down or to put their behavior into boxes. One thing which you can be sure of is that, some of the time, they seek happiness. They often get this 'happiness' through their interactions and relationships with other humans.

In a New World environment there is less and less time to build new relationships and partnerships. *The emotional roller coaster that the New World creates demands that you are either emotionally resilient or you work with people who have enough of the fun and humor bit to counter the emotional lows.* Because there is less and less time to form relationships and more relevantly, to maintain relationships. The memory of each meeting, each phone call, each contact, must last much longer. It must linger more effectively. It *becomes increasingly important that you delight the people you work with.* On the other hand you are also aware that you, and those you work with, are under relentless pressure to improve performance. Guess what? All this means that we come to *value people who challenge us in a supportive way.*"

"The flip side of the coin is also heads," he says cryptically. "You seek the same interaction from people, whether they are customer or supplier. And, you seek the same behavior from them as you offer, in delighting and challenging them. *'Delight and challenge'* is a special case of *'overdemand and overpay'*."

"What do you mean special case?" asks the Empowering Manager.

"How would you feel if I offered to double your pay?"

He starts to reply, "Brill..." and then he gets the message. "Got it," he says nodding decisively.

"Yes, if you think about it for a while, you will discover that it is two ways of saying the same thing."

The Sixthe Rule
MAKE TIME FIT!

Either this man is dead... or my watch has stopped

Groucho Marx

"Do you recognize this sequence?" He puts up a transparency which says:
- work harder (piece rate)
- prioritize
- work even harder (productivity)
- work smarter
- reinvent your work processes
- stretch yourself.

"If you do, then you are just about ready for the New World addition. You see, as the world has accelerated, time has stayed constant. The sequence described on the transparency goes from; measuring what work is being done in a given time, through choosing to lead on one piece of work rather than another, through coming up with faster and faster ways of doing the work, through inventing clever ways of doing and managing the work, through actually changing the work activities crammed in, through to filling your life entirely with working night and day. By this point your life is getting really sad. All other responsibilities, opportunities for fun and simply wasting time have been significantly squeezed. '*Making time fit*', making time meet **your** needs is the way you need to think in the New World."

Make Time = Parallel

"I tend to use a method I call FOLDING. Folding is essentially about making time parallel. With folding you find as many opportunities as possible for allowing more than one thing to happen at a time. For example, it is no longer unusual to see people driving whilst talking on the phone. That to me, is an example of folding. Increasingly these days I see fewer and fewer people waiting by a printer for a document to print out, usually they are doing something else. I see more people making phone calls with the handset on hook, using their loud-speakers, so that they can be working on other things right up to the point when the person they want to speak to comes on-line.

In business organizational terms the same message applies. Are there concurrencies which can be exploited? A great one I heard about was that of getting delivery van drivers to collect and update orders for the next delivery."

Everything Has Sell-by Dates

"Recently, I was working with an organization which had begun to tie itself in knots. The reason, it seemed, was that the organization was undergoing a lot of change and as a result there were many projects running concurrently. At the same time the high levels of change were making the senior management nervous, with the net result that they were demanding ongoing reports from all the project leaders and line managers on the progress of their projects. Asking for progress reports makes sense. Well, if that's on its own. But, the senior managers were also trying to predict the resource levels which would be required in the near future and for this they demanded forward forecasts and plans. Again not unreasonable but given the levels of change many of the plans quickly became obsolete. As a result, the resource planning was continually wrong. The reaction of the senior managers to this was to ask for more progress reports and then occasionally haul an unlucky project leader into their offices, show their original plans and then 'chew them out' for not meeting the original schedules. Can you guess what the net result was?"

"Low morale," suggests the Organizational Developer.

Franck nods approvingly. "And, apart from the resignation of one of the best project leaders, anything else?"

"False reports?" suggests the Benchmarker.

"Precisely! Contingencies big enough to hide the costs of the channel tunnel in, plus an apparent critical lack of resources in the short and long-term future. Stalemate! The solution we came up with in the end was a planning and resource scheduling process with a sell-by date. Each plan and report said in the right hand corner, 'This plan is valid until...' Net result, project leaders who felt once again empowered to tell the truth, realistic resource and progress forecasts and a senior management who could again sleep through the night.

Do It Now!

'*Do it now!*' is about many things. The first is, it is about inventory. If you, like I, were taught about how to be an efficient and effective manager in the Old World, I guess you were taught to make lists and prioritize? Making lists of tasks involves thinking about work as a sequence and not as 'folded time'(see above). One of my favorite examples of '*Do it now!*' also involves some folding. It is the practice I use often of writing proposals **during** the client meeting. You know that you are planning a meeting in order to work out and agree what the two parties intend to do. You know that the client will need a document to show to the rest of their team in order to gain understanding and agreement, so '*Do it now!*'. I take to the meeting an outline electronic format of the document we will end up with as the meeting proceeds. I take notes onto the computer immediately into the appropriate section. 'Who will be participating in the continuous learning course?' They tell me. I type it into the section titled 'participants'. As the meeting draws to a close, I ask for a few minutes to do a spell check and to check the formatting of the document. And then we read it together or I print it out (enter Meatspace ugh!) for us to read and check it together. Any corrections are agreed and the document is corrected and taken away at once. '*Do it now!*' *is an antidote to the speed at which the New World moves*. I know it's true that some challenges if left, tend to mature into better opportunities and that a '*Do it now!*' approach also risks work being done and then the world moves on, needs and requirements become clearer, something else was needed and the work has been wasted. But I guess it is unlikely that the Old World or efficiencies apply and perhaps the slightly wasteful *And!* of '*Do it now!*' *gives you a better chance of being in pole position if the race starts*.

I started this discussion by saying that the first focus was on inventory. I guess you were just about to ask me how '*Do it now!*' links to inventory since I haven't mentioned it since I started."

"It's obvious," says the Re-engineer. "Once you *'Do it now!'* there is no duration to tasks since they are tackled or deleted as soon as they arise. The normal build up of a back log is avoided. The inventory is reduced."

"Great," he congratulates. "I couldn't have said it better myself. I guess that what I would add is that by using *'Do it now!'* there is less future inventory of work to manage, as a result *you save the time you would otherwise spend on prioritizing and managing the lists of tasks.* It also gives you more degrees of freedom in what the future can look like for you, since it is not predetermined by the list of tasks in the queue. But best of all, remember the uncertainty which the New World brings, *it stops you suffering increasing uncertainty* as the New World obliterates the original demand for actions you have held and managed as inventory for a while. It allows you to look to the future with more certainty.

The flip side of *'Do it now!'* is to *develop a decision process which eliminates activities which you never intend to deal with.* At least not in your current lifetime. I think, things like the high speed 'open – delete' process I'm sure you use with your e-mails, is an example. And if the task is too big to complete in the very near future you may wish to consider the rule, *Chunk it or Junk it!*"

Back from the Future

Franck walks slowly across the room, sits on the edge of the table on the right hand side of the U, hauls himself backwards so that now his feet dangle lackadaisically inches above the floor. He breathes in deeply and then exhales, "Do you have any particularly obnoxious customers? I don't mean ones who are off their rocker, but obnoxiously demanding ones. Ones who ask you to provide goods and services you can't possibly acheive are ones who are unrealistic in their expectations of what they want from you. The sort you might laugh and joke about, to relieve the tension of their unreasonableness?"

Heads nod and there is one verbal reply, "Yes we had one the other week who was asking about next day delivery for a product we normally promise for a week. He couldn't seem to understand that we had to order parts and then produce what he wanted."

Franck nods sagely. "Yep, that's one all right. The bane of the Benchmarker who is using customer satisfaction as a performance measure. You get to 90% satisfactions and then get stuck because of people like that. It's very tempting to leave them out of the survey all together. It makes sense. After all they're off the scale and most likely not part of the segment you are interested in. You don't know where to classify the comments they make at the bottom of their forms in the 'Any other comments?' section."

He pauses looking for a reaction. Both the Customer-Focused Manager and the Business Benchmarker are nodding vigorously. "I have some very bad news for you. These customers, *these obnoxious customers are far more important to you than all the 'satisfieds' put together*. The obnoxious customer provides what one of my friends describes as a *future echo*. Something like a shadow cast backwards through time from the future giving a hint of the shape and size of what is yet to come. The obnoxious customer is often simply a winged messenger warning of things of come. The obnoxious customer provides the vision. In reality of course, relying on the obnoxious customer to provide your organization's vision is a really risky business. They could just as easily tell the vision to one of your competitors. Providing the future echoes for your own organization is actually one of the few things you would not ever wish to outsource, a real core capability. And yet, this is the very thing which organizations seem to stumble on, the vision thing. I believe that the reason that they stumble, is they try to build this complete picture but in **words**. *If you really want to build a vision, avoid using lengthy wordy descriptions. Use pictures but paint those pictures as if they were reality, paint the future echoes not the actual future*. What would an obnoxious customer demand? What would an obnoxious CEO demand? What would an obnoxious salesperson demand? What would an obnoxious regulator demand? *By working your way round your stakeholder group considering their future echoes you get a sense of an appropriate vision for the near term*. And, of course, in the New World the near term is an awfully long time."

"I hear what you say," says the Merged Chief Executive loudly, "but even if we could use your technique to build a vision which was the *most likely expression of the present in the future*, it would still be of little use. You seem to have forgotten that *in the New World it is much easier to create a strategy than it is to bring it to a successful conclusion.* It's easier to listen to demands than it is to actually implement what you intended."

"You're right," says Franck conceding, "but even then, even if you develop a great strategy the idea of *'Back from the future!'* can be used again.' *'Back from the future!'* is the basis of an approach to planning I invented a couple of years ago. It's a method called 'Sticky Steps'." He walks across to his pile of slides, rummages through them for a while and then with a triumphant flourish retrieves two acetates, the first of which he places on the overhead projector. *The less certain the future is the more important it is that a realistic bridge is built from here to there.* **Sticky Steps** *is a structured brainstorm which allows you to brainstorm a possible route, hopefully* **the most probable route,** *from the future to today.* The slide reads:

STICKY STEPS™

Part 1: Working out the steps

Step 1   Try to work out the 'what' of your chunk. If you are leading an open project, just guess the 'what'. You can change it later.

Step 2   Write on a large sheet, flip chart or wall whiteboard, "in order to have..."

Step 3   Write down the what of your chunk on a post-it note. Start with a **verb** in the **past tense**. For example, "installed business process re-engineering".

Step 4   Continue with the sentence you have written down on the large sheet. Write "We would have had to have..." or "We must have!!!"

Step 5   Imagine that you have actually completed the chunk and you are looking backwards in time. Write on a post-it note anything you can imagine you would have had to have done.

Step 6   Place the post-it on the board underneath the sentence to the right hand side.

Step 7   Ask yourself if there is anything else.

Step 8   If there is, write it down on another post-it note.

Step 9   Go back to Step 7 until there is nothing further to add.

Step 10 Choose one of the stickies and use it to replace the original "what" (at the end of "in order to have..." place the original "what" in the top right hand corner of the board).

Step 11 Now move all the other yellow stickies to the left hand side of the board.

Step 12 Go back to step 5.

Step 13 Repeat this loop until the stickies have TASKS written on them. TASKS, that is, things which you could wake up on Monday morning and decide you were going to do, and just do.

Step 14 Move the tasks to the top right hand corner of the board.

Step 15 Discard all the stickies you generated in the loop getting to the tasks.

Step 16 Take the next sticky from the bottom left hand side.

Step 17 Go back to Step 5.

Step 18 When you have worked your way through all the loops the first part of the process is over.

Part 2: Gaining buy-in, communicating, scheduling tasks

Step 1 Invite the key stakeholders to part one of the sticky steps.
Remind them to bring their diaries.

Step 2 Carry out Part 1 of the Sticky Steps with the key stakeholders.

Step 3 On a second board write all the names of your key stakeholders vertically down the left hand side.

Step 4 Write a time axis along the top horizontally.
Choose the appropriate time frame for the type of change:

Closed – actual dates/times up to the final date or drop-dead date;

Open – three columns labelled "THIS WEEK" (or MONTH), "NEXT WEEK" (or MONTH) and "SOON". Choose the time scale to represent how far you can see in the fog. If you can see the next month with certainty, use the one-week scale. If you can see the next six months, use the month scale.

Step 5 Number all the post-its with tasks on them (any numbering system will do as long as it is simple).

Step 6 Lift a sticky off the first board and read it out to the group.

Step 7 Ask "who should do this?" Wait for a volunteer or for someone to be volunteered.

Step 8 Ask "when should it be done?", "when should it start?" If there are answers write them on the top right hand side of the post-it.

Step 9 Ask "who passes you the baton?" If you know and it is obvious, write on the left hand corner who passes the baton (and the number of the sticky, if known).

Step 10 Ask "who do you pass the baton to?" If you know and it is obvious, write on the right hand corner the person the baton is passed to (and the number of the sticky is known)

Step 11 Transfer a sticky from the first board to the second board.
Place it against the name and time.

Step 12 Ask the person involved in the sticky "have you got that?"
Encourage them to put it in their diary.

Step 13 Go back to Step 6 and repeat until all the post-its have been transferred.

Step 14 Look at the board. Ask people what they think their workload is. If they say that it is more than 70%, insert a time buffer. Use your judgement to work out how long the time buffer should be.

Step 15 Look at the board. Wherever more than one activity must be complete before the next activities can be started, insert a time buffer. Use your judgement to work out how long the time buffer should be.

Step 16 (For neatness maniacs only) get the schedule drawn up neatly.

He talks the group through the method. And then offers them each yellow sticky pads and suggests that they try it out. Fifteen minutes later and the walls of the room look as if they've been hit by a yellow blizzard.

"I guess in the best traditions of *'Do it Now!'* it must be lunchtime Now!"

Rule the Sevenf
CHUNK IT OR JUNK IT!

Learn to see things backwards, inside out and upside down.
from the Tao Te Ching of Lao Tzu

"The problem with change is how we think about it. What I'd like you to do, is to think about how you might represent change in the Old World." He pauses expectantly. Unfortunately Franck's gaze is met by a sea of uncomprehending stares so he expresses his instructions more clearly. "OK I'd like you to take a piece of paper and fold it in half, down the long edge. Good. Now what I'd like you to do is to write on the left hand side, Old World. And guess what I'd like you to write on the right hand side? All right, now I would like you to create a pictorial or graphical representation of 'Change' as you perceive it in the two worlds. Pretend you are a famous pretentious artist. You are aware that you may have to explain to an adoring public what your picture means." Now there is silence for two minutes as the group draw furiously and not so furiously on the sheets in front of them. "All done?"

The last pen is returned to rest on the table. "Now I would like you to hold up your pictures so that all your colleagues can see." It's amazing. The pattern is almost completely consistent. On the left Old World side the general theme is of arrows, straight lines and circles and for the more exotic, the left hand profile of a flight of stairs. The right hand sides are less uniform, unless you describe a series of pictures containing squiggles, curves, non-geometric shapes, stick people lying on their backs, toes up, as consistent. Consistent perhaps only in theme. He grabs a plastic ruler. "I guess this is what happens in the Old World," he says, bending the ruler slightly as he demonstrates extrapolation. "And in the New World we are pulled up and down and in several directions. *A single strategy which only works when all the parts work, is far to rigid to survive,*" he says and with that he bends both ends of the ruler downwards whilst pushing upward with his thumb. The ruler rewards this effort by disintegrating into several pieces with a resounding snap. It seems a waste but the point is made.

"I'll tell you my favorite example of a strategy which is made flexible through modularisation. Have you noticed how Motorway service stations are built these days? In the good old days the whole complex would be constructed at the same time, motel, petrol station, shops and so on. What do they do now? They build the petrol station, and the toilets," he adds with a smile, "for incentive. Then they build the shops, then the accommodation. Each activity, chunked. *The whole change is broken into bite-sized manageable pieces. Each activity capable of providing a benefit on its own. Each activity developed and delivered at a time to suit the demand. It's almost as if the strategy itself were modular. Each module delivering some additional and incremental value.*"

He pauses waiting for questions. Unfortunately there aren't any and he looks slightly confused, as if he is surprised that he has communicated effectively. He continues slowly and obviously reluctantly. "I always feel that if you drew the cash flows for the two cases, in one you would end up with a long period of spend followed by a long period of revenue, whilst in the New World version the spend is followed by the revenue, almost in parallel."

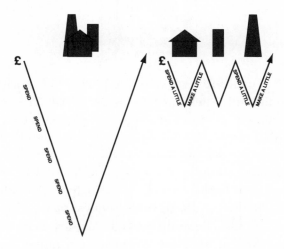

He draws two diagrams on the flip chart and explains, "I call this a 'V' strategy and this other one a 'W' strategy. Are they both long term?" The Strategist replies, "Yes I guess so, they both seem to end at the same point of implementation so I guess the net result must be equally strategic."

"But if it was **your** money, and you lived in the New World, a world where a year is now a very long time, which one would you go for?" His question is a no brainer, the Strategist grins broadly.

"I guess the key to success in using modular thinking is deciding how to modularize. He walks to the back of the room stopping in front of a large wooden storage unit. He opens the left door. An "Aha" emanates from his lips. He is obviously delighted to have found the thing he was looking for. It appears to be a deck of cards. The cards are held together by a paper loop on which the word 'Modulorama' appears in bright red. Franck is now dealing out four cards to each participant. He looks stern and very, very serious. He gives instructions. "I would like you," he says, "to arrange these cards in the correct sequence; it's very difficult, you have five minutes." The seriousness with which he delivers the message makes all the participants set off energetically to work.

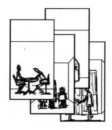

After about 13 seconds there is a muffled "Huh" of bewilderment. A second later another participant repeats the noise. Now it's a chorus. Franck is standing at the front of the group grinning, very amused at some secret joke.

"They're interchangeable!" exclaims the Empowering Manager, still baffled.

"Precisely. But what *makes* them interchangeable?"

"I guess the interface is almost exactly the same. The artist has *freedom everywhere except* at the carefully defined and fixed *connection points.*"

"Fantastic, you have explained that more succinctly than I possibly could. It is this same thinking you must apply to the unit structures of the organization, for example your teams, If you operate with a team structure there must be fixed link points. In one organization I worked with, we invented a team based structure with each team having commonality through what we described as mini-boards. Roughly the same small group of executives who kept the fixed points fixed. Same board, just plug in and out, the team. I'm afraid of course that with human beings it's not always so easy. You can apply this thinking to product design also very effectively, you will already have noticed the trend in many manufactured products to use similar connectors, such as kettle leads, or the way the dashboard or console of your car has those blank 'spaces', blanked-off rectangles where some gizmo could have been inserted, I'm assuming that you don't have the topmost top of the range. If you do, you gain an extra two tons of weight with the 'gizmos from hell' version." He grins.

"If the financial measures that your organization uses are the only common fixed points, you will find yourself at a severe disadvantage because the *financial results measure the* **outcome** *of business activities* **not** *the actual effectiveness of the activities as they are happening. They provide historic information which is static.* That is why it has become fashionable to measurement approaches which cover a wider range of both inputs and processes. Techniques such as balanced scorecards and total quality models help identify the effectiveness of a wider range of activities. But be careful, think about the cards." He stresses, "They work well because *although there are fixed points there are few fixed points.* Imagine that we had defined twenty or thirty necessary conditions at the interface. For a start the artist would have had less freedom. Far more of the picture would be dictated by interface. A green line next to a blue line stops you from drawing a tree. And the artist would spend so much time making sure that the interface fitted that they would have less time to think about the overall picture.

Simply by adding a few features points, order emerges irrespective of the actual range and scope of opportunities. *It's almost as if by making sure that things are **loosely linked** to each other, loosely coupled, it **creates** order and **calm**."*

Modularize

"I guess the other reason that *'Chunk it or Junk it!'* appeals, is that it can be applied to a wide range of situations. Let's take for example, the way in which we have thought about opportunities for growth. One of the most common models we know is this one." On the flip chart he sketches a cube which is then filled in. He asks, "Is this familiar?"

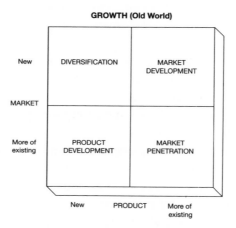

GROWTH (Old World)

"OK, so I can get this to work for me in a more stable and linear environment. Of course I can, the sell-by date of any particular offer is very long. You can make megadosh by selling the same thing, unchanged, as an offer to an increasing number of people. But what happens in a rapidly changing environment? It becomes *increasingly high risk to build each product from scratch.* During one of the tales we heard last night, I think it was yours," he says pointing at the Customer-Focused Manager, "you said:

'I guess in the New World, the concept of product life cycle is probably already dead. Look, for example, at the introduction of telecommunications into Eastern Europe, a life cycle model would not explain the simultaneous development of land-based, digital and cable systems.'

"I guess the first New World trick is to modularize your concept of what you are offering potential customers."

"What do you mean?" asks the Customer-Focused Manager.

"Why do we pay any attention to customers?"

"Because without customers, you have no business," replies the Customer-Focused Manager.

"And why is that?"

"Because they are important."

"And **why** are they important?" asks Franck, in a tone which does little to betray the fact that he feels that getting to this answer is like pulling out a tooth.

"Because they are the source of revenue."

"Precisely!" he exclaims, relieved that the interrogation has ended at least for now. "And why would anyone part with their money to you?"

"I don't know. Perhaps they will, if you give them something in return."

"Anything in particular you need to offer them?"

"Well, I guess if you offer them something tangible, like a product, they would pay for it."

"Anything else you could offer them to make them part with their money?"

"You could provide a service," he says flatly.

"And what do you mean by a service?"

He thinks for a while and is about to answer when the Informatized Manager slips in with, *"advice, information, help, personal support."*

The Customer-Focused Manager nods in agreement.

"Great answer," responds Franck. "Is there anything else?"

"Not that I can think of," replies the Informatized Manager.

"Aha!" exclaims Franck pointing to the shirt worn by the Re-engineer. "I have a friend who had a shirt like that. The Re-engineer's shirt is plain orange, the only distinguishing feature being a motif on the breast pocket." It's obvious that he's pointing at the motif. The motif depicts a bird, wings half-stretched, with beligerent red beady eyes. It's some sort of 'Phoenix rising from the flames' theme. He says, "My friend was very pleased with his shirt. I asked him how much it cost and he told me it cost £100. Now, of course, to me, a poor teacher, that sounds like a fortune. To me a shirt costs, oh, no more than £20. So my conclusion is very simple. Shirt without motif, £20. Shirt with motif," he crosses his wrists and makes a flapping movement with his hands to illustrate the bird's wings, "£100. Therefore motif costs... £80."

All the participants start laughing at the cock-eyed logic.

He feigns bewilderment, "What? What?" and then he grins. "So the third thing people will pay you for is?"

"A brand," says the Customer-Focused Manager, as if s/he'd known the answer all along.

"Yes a brand, an aura, an idea in their minds. Amazingly people will pay good money for an aura, an idea. You see, *what you offer people as an exchange has three types of components. The aura, the product and the service*. You can tweak each or all to deliver what the customer needs. He turns to the flipchart and draws:

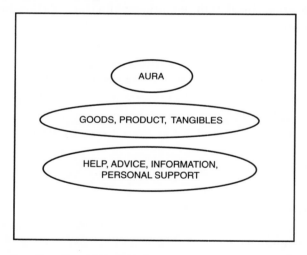

"I believe that in the New World, in order to keep meeting the changing demands existing and potential customers make on us, it is pretty important to break what you offer into the three elements. That way you can think about altering one of the elements at a time, to give you additional benefits, without being forced back to the drawing board to create from scratch each time. You see, if it has become *increasingly high risk to build each product from scratch*, it makes sense for our offer to evolve a bit at a time. Some of this we already recognize. A brand extension, or aura extension is about keeping that module the same and then altering the product or service to match. A product extension is about altering the aura or the service element to allow additional offerings and a service extension is about altering the aura or the product content of an offering to allow additional people to part with their money. In the Old World environment organizations would often describe themselves as being in manufacturing or service. That, I hope you can now see, is completely irrelevant. We have brand management for managing the aura and product development and management for looking after the product part of the offering, but few organizations have a *capability to look after the service module of the offer. And yet in reality, that is one area which is often harder to copy and so has a longer shelf-life in providing a sustainable competitive advantage to the organization.* Bizarre. And how do we integrate these activities? The New World demands that the links between these different parts of the offer be designed simultaneously. I now think about market development like this:" He scribbles on the next flip chart.

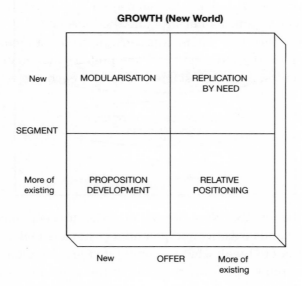

GROWTH (New World)

Break? Five minutes? Come back with your thoughts on how you could modularize your current offerings?"

Make it Self-similar

"The best thing about the old magic symbol, for hierarchies, was that you only had to explain it once. Franck is frantically drawing the familiar 'rake' design on a flip chart. You see, if the organization grew you just repeated the symbol again and it was infinitely scaleable. Furthermore it meant the same thing over and over. One of the problems of the New World is that the added complexity of the situations we have to cope with encourage us to deal with each situation or challenge as a 'one-off'. You must resist this temptation. Wherever possible make things self-similar. By that I mean, *personal ground rules* or values should *be reflected in team ground rules* which should, in turn, be reflected *in process ground rules* and finally in the *organization's ground rules*. Some people would argue that the reverse should be true, that organizational ground rules should be reflected in team and process ground rules. I don't really care which way you work it, as long as you only have to explain it once. Because at each level the input is self-similar. The same applies to the ways we represent aspects of organizational structure. Perhaps one of the best self-similar structures I've seen was designed by a Scandinavian manufacturer for the organization of the projects they managed. The organization used a lozenge shape to describe each project."

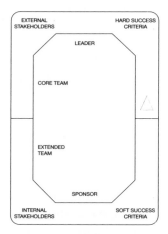

"This basic format was used at the task level, the sub-project level, the strategic level. The project triangle was used to ensure consistent focus on timeliness, financial aspects or specific deliverables. A dot was placed at a point on the triangle to show the focus. All team participants were then aware of trade-offs and could be effectively empowered. This is a structure I often use myself:

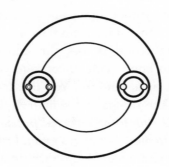

And another:

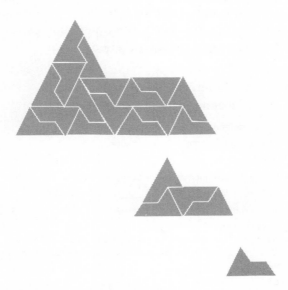

Another approach I've used effectively is to structure all internal documents in the same way. A structure I really like is to use the headings..." he lists bullet points on the chart and then explains:

- Purpose – what does the document hope to achieve
- Principles – the key ground rules to watch out for, plus reference to any other organizational principles

- Process – how the decision/implementation is to happen (know-how, see re-inventing information)
- People – who the stakeholders are and why.

*The format is **self-similar** across the organization and is almost task or activity independent.*

Review Too Often

"As we apply '***Chunk it or Junk it!***', the need to constantly figure out how we're doing and what needs to be done next grows tremendously. In the New World you can almost never have too many reviews. ***The reviews you perform need to be timely and fast***, not like the post-mortems of the Old World. The overall emphasis must be on learning, not on assigning blame or looking for scapegoats. The first stage of the process is to time box activities and then, almost like a slow motion film to step through frame by frame harvesting learning. I use a method called 'Action Replay." Franck now passes round a single sheet handout titled unsurprisingly, 'Action Replay':

ACTION REPLAY™

Step 1   ASK WHEN we started/finished the period under review.

Decide the time period that the review is to cover…

Step 2   ASK WHAT have we done?

Start with the most recent memories. For example, "what went right/wrong yesterday?"

Step 3   ASK HOW yesterday's outcomes arose.

For example, "How did we get it to work so well?"

Step 4   ASK WHO was involved?
The stakeholders will have the best idea of what actually happened. For example "Who set it up this way?" Be careful with this question that you are not seeming to apportion blame.

Step 5   ASK WHERE it went right or wrong.

Establish the key steps which got us here.

Step 6   ASK WHY it happened.

If the answer is complex, draw a bubble diagram.

Step 7   Summarise what you have learned as a general principle and make sure that all the other reviewers understand it.

Step 8   Make sure that any actions arising from what you have learned are owned.

Step 9   Repeat steps for the previous day.

Rule the Aigthe
MOVE ALL CONSTRAINTS TO MEATSPACE

> *Who controls the past, ran the Party slogan, controls the future: who controls the present controls the past.*
>
> George Orwell

"Cyberspace," Franck announces, using an imitation of the voice which is always used for the voice-over descriptions of trailers of cheap 'coming shortly to a cinema near you' films, the deep gravelly tone nicknamed in the industry, 'The Voice Of God', "Cyberspace the final frontier!"

The participants are looking at him as if he has finally gone mad.

"I know you think I've lost the plot, but I haven't. **We only know that Meatspace exists because we can touch it. Cyberspace we only ever interpret**. The sounds coming down the phone line, as a voice, the black and white pixels on a computer screen, as a page and so on. The great thing about cyberspace is the speed with which the parts can move. Look, why does any business not make an infinite amount of money?" He pauses and then commits the sin he had promised not to, for the third time that day he answers his own question. "It's surely because 'something' holds it back. That 'something' is a **constraint**. Constraints limit our ability to deliver what we wish to. If you accept that *every process has constraints*, then the question I need to ask you is, 'Where would you want the constraint to be?' If it was entirely your choice 'Where would you wish the constraint to be?'. Would you want it in your own control? Or in someone else's?" This time he waits for an answer.

"Could you repeat the question again?" asks the Re-engineer.

"Sure. If you accept that every process has constraints... where would you want the constraint to be? Would you want it in your own control or in someone else's?"

Phrased like that, the answer is quite obvious. A business whose constraints lie in the market will find itself with over-capacity and unable to plan but always be driven by the marketplace. Or perhaps if a regulatory body holds the business constraints, they will find themselves forced into constant re-negotiations and requests for policy changes. Definitely, you wish constraints to be in your own control. The Re-engineer says so.

"Good. Now how about this one? Would you rather have your constraints in cyberspace, for example the difficulty of retrieving data or a slow computer system which results in long queues of customers or unbilled work, or would you rather be constrained by a Meatspace issue, such as the actual speed of installation or the managerial time available for managing the business?"

This is less obvious. There is a very, very pregnant silence.

"Why don't we break into buzz groups to discuss it and see what we come up with?" A second later the room is abuzz. At the end of the group discussion Franck concludes, "*Any organization seeking to compete on speed must move as much as possible of its operations into cyberspace*. Think about the impact this has on strategies which have been pursued for decades such as centralizing production or making use of centers of excellence. As soon as the information flow lines stop being the same as the reporting and control routes, certain key people become very important. *It is by finding and empowering the people* who fall *at the nodes* of the *communication* that *we* really *get the best out of cyberspace* whilst *keeping* the *constraints* firmly *in Meatspace and firmly in our control.*"

Re-invent your Information

The problem with cyberspace is that, just like the lower reaches of real space, it's full of space junk. You don't believe me.? Surf the net for a day and see, or even simpler, work out how much of your e-mail today was really useful. My personal belief is that most people don't really know what information is or what it's for." He pauses with this challenging statement but all he receives is agreement.

"Yeah, makes sense, all the stuff I get copied in on," says the Organization Development Manager. "In my organization we seem to use e-mail as a way of avoiding doing any work. You get a task, first thing you do is e-mail everyone and do nothing. If anyone chases you,

you can claim that you've e-mailed key stakeholders and are waiting for their input." Heads nod in agreement, but not vigorously. They remember the tale from the night before, and fear they are covering the same ground.

Franck looks disappointed at this flat reaction. He had wanted more discussion.

"I spend the first half hour every day opening e-mails with attachments and trashing them," adds the Organisational Developer hopefully.

Franck seems to brighten. "Why do you think that they are sending you stuff which is of no value to you?"

"I guess it's like we heard yesterday, *'information and data are not the same thing, you want answers, you want information. Information is the answer to the question asked. If you are not asking the question then anything they send you is useless to you. It's just data'.*"

"I agree," he says, "information is part of a living system your organization needs to rediscover. You remember earlier someone mentioned attachments?"

"It was me, I was complaining about them. And how long it takes you to open them up, only to discover that they are in the wrong format or version or add nothing to your thinking," said the Global Communicator.

"But tell me about the attachments. Why are they sending you those?" asks Franck.

"I guess they expect me to use them to work out the **actions** I need to take."

"So some information is about actions?"

"Yes."

"And some tells you what has happened?"

"Yeah."

"So are those two types of information different?"

"I don't understand what you mean"

"*Information enabling you to take an action* versus *information which tells you about what has happened?*"

"Oh I see. You mean, is the reason that I need the information different? I guess it is."

"And does that mean you want to get your hands on a different type of information?" Franck stares accusingly at the Benchmarker.

"I guess so," says the Global Communicator with a slight shrug.

Franck has turned his attention to a flip chart, and even now, is marking up and labeling a diagram.

"I'd hoped it wouldn't be four but there seem to be four types of information. He explains why he had wished for a different outcome.

"Four types seems a bit trite. Everybody has models with groups of four."

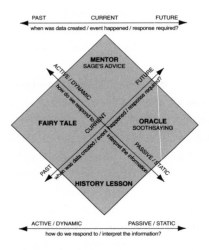

The first type of answer is the type which organizations are usually very keen on. It is the answer to the question *"What happened?" It is information where **the data** required has been **created and collected** sometime **in the past**.* As a rule, the data simply records an event or parameter. It tells you about the **content** of a historic activity. A bit like swotting up the dates in a **history lesson**. Most organizations are obsessed and swamped with this sort of information. What were last month's sales? (or even next month's sales projections? remember, the targets were probably set six months ago even though the event hasn't occurred yet), market share information, number of employees, their names, hobbies and dog/cat preferences are all this type of **content** information. Organizations tend to focus upon one type of content information, the attributes. This includes numbers of units, perhaps color, and so on. The attributes act as a shorthand for content information, but going back to the history lesson you may know the date the *Mayflower* sailed and how many people were on board but asked to describe one of the sails you may want to resort to another type of content information, *form* information. Form information answers questions on just that, '*What is it?*' the form of an object. Form data describes the roughness, the fiber content, the actual shape (they weren't exact rectangles). *Content information, as attributes, is brilliantly compatible with computer cyberspace.* It easily fits into databases and spreadsheets. **Form** can also be stored in computer cyberspace but not very efficiently. For a start, a translation of **Form** to numbers has to happen. Just think about how big even graphics files are. And then you need to go out and buy an enormous hard disk."

"You mean form information is less efficient to store?" asks the Re-engineer.

"Infinitely, especially information on real objects. Storing the Form information, even on something as important as your Phoenix shirt is a major task."

"Perhaps that's why we have concentrated on content attribute information," suggests the Informatized Manager.

"I agree. And we're brilliant at it but just remember, as customers become more demanding, **Form** gives us another dimension to explore. The seats in your car could be not only gray leather but soft gray leather or warm gray leather. Two different types of information linked to two different questions. 'What color are the seats? What is the seat like?'"

The Customer-Focused Manager is scribbling furiously.

"Let's look at something else. Go back to the earlier part of our discussion, when we were talking about organizations' obsession with attribute content data. If you think about the sales meeting where you were asked for last month's sales, you may also remember being asked why the figure is so brilliant (in your case), abysmal (in mine). I bet you embarked on a **fairy tale**. 'Once upon a time in a market far far away, there was a group of customers who formed a segment. Now in this segment, there was a need for a product. But because there was no product, the people in the segment felt very sad. One day, a sales knight came along, etcetera, What you are now describing is still in the past, but now you are *explaining how it came about,* you are describing some of the softer aspects such *as how the people were feeling, the behavior* of the various stakeholders within the **fairy tale**. Of course, in your case, the fairy tale is what **actually** happened. (In my fairy tale it's all made up.) Often, the discussion then moves to

'What could it be?'. This type of information is *predictive*. It's like consulting an **oracle** or **soothsayer**."

"Are you suggesting that we look in a crystal ball for business answers?" asks the Strategist.

Franck grins in response. "I always think of the story of that Greek geezer, Croesus, Emperor type, King of Lydia, I think ages ago, who consulted the oracle at Delphi which told him that if he attacked the Persians, a great empire would be destroyed. So he attacked and **his** empire was destroyed. What do you think that the oracle was actually trying to tell him?"

"Perhaps that both parties had fully entrenched positions and that when a pair like that go to war it usually ends in destruction for one of them," the Strategist replies insightfully.

"Precisely. *Predictive information is about patterns*. It's about *recognizing the general from the specific*. It's like what we are doing now, using last night's tales to discover rules."

The Strategist nods, smiling.

"Now let's go back to your discussion in real life. After you've told them the fairy tale and you've made some predictions about the common patterns in similar situations, my guess is the conversation turned to *'How could it come about?'* Am I right? Is that what happens? I guess the challenge is to use all four types of information. Each on its own is useful but together, and only together, do they provide the learning and action essential for success in a New World which is also a Virtual space world.

To be an effective New World manager you must develop your capability to exploit all four types of information. I have a very simple exercise. It's a simple audit of where you invest your time to gather information."
He draws on the flip chart a diamond similar to the previous one only this time he leaves it blank. He instructs, "What I'd like you to do is to think through a day at work, either a specific day or typical day, or even a meeting, and on this diagram let's see where most time was spent. I'll tell you what, why don't you do it on your own first, and then we can discuss it as a group?"

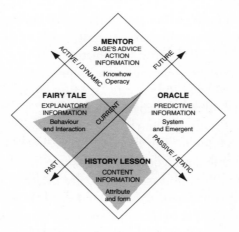

They share their reviews. Some people have shaded in the diagram to represent the focus, others have placed ticks or crosses representing each topic or hour. The result is depressing. Franck suggests a short 'comfort break'.

Stay DIGITAL in Cyberspace

"This one is a no-brainer. In Virtual Space world there is nothing more effective than staying digital. Whatever you do, *avoid moving from Space World into Here and Now World*. If it's in a digital format keep it there, don't print it out. But staying digital is more than just about the medium you use for storing and transporting information, it is also the basis of a New World strategy. '*Stay digital*' should affect your investment strategy. If you are in manufacturing, where should you be manufacturing? Should you move products to "centers of manufacturing excellence"? Or should you move the information to where the materials are? An interesting example I saw recently, from a utility company, was the use of locals with head-mounted cameras through which pictures of their plant, cameras… a bit like a miner's helmet but with a camera instead of a lamp." Now he is miming what he is describing. "Trouble shooting and inspection could be beamed from the camera. It meant that an 'expert' somewhere in the world could observe, guide and provide the know-how for dealing with problems as they came down the cable to their screen."

Stop Communicating!

"Eight people meet in a darkened room for half a day. Adding up the cost of salaries, associated costs, e.g., the company cars, costs of traveling to and from the venue and the costs of the venue, the total amount of money spent on that half day comes to just under £1500. What you need to know is that the profit margin for the organization is 10%. So if this meeting is anything over and above the normal day-to-day stuff of business, guess how much additional sales revenue will have to be generated, just to stay square? Yes, you can do the sums too, £15,000: frightening isn't it? And yet, all over the world, people invest in a form of activity called face-to-face meetings. Bizarre!"

While the participants are reeling under their own thoughts of the implications of the bizarre way in which their organizations are spending their money, Franck headbutts them again. "Another strange thing. Most people believe that the way to get a message over is to communicate it. Now, you may know, that the advertising industry employs many of the world's most creative minds and puts them to work for days and weeks crafting communication messages. These messages, these beautifully constructed, scientifically validated messages in the right color and tone, then have to be repeated to the average citizen a good half dozen times before they even notice it. And then another half dozen times before they understand it. And maybe are biased to respond. *And we only notice the communication if the **message** both **matches** the **medium** through which it is delivered* *and matches our perceptions at the time.* I remember reading about a company which seven years ago produced a mobile phone which was smaller than a packet of cigarettes, approximately credit card sized. This was in the days when most mobile phones weighed as much as a large full briefcase and were about the size of a pair of household bricks. And yet sales never took off, because people watching the television advertisement didn't recognize it as a **real** product, they just ignored the message, dismissing it as a James Bond type, fictional gizmo. Perhaps the medium was wrong or the perception was wrong. Tell me, what chance do we, with our busy schedules, normal levels of creativity, lack of time to beautifully craft our messages, what chance do we stand in trying to use communication, especially written communication or even spoken communication (without the sexy pulsating backing track to underpin the message)? What chance do we stand of ever having an effective communication process for the whole organization? And yet the management gurus and consultants have convinced us that this is the one way to develop strategies and create the changes we need to succeed with in the New World. Just work out the additional sales you need to support a meeting of 100 staff and see whether the communication is worth that much. What do you think? Don't you get it? Meetings are in Meatspace." He grins. "If you *'move all your constraints to Meatspace'* you will do your best to *use that constraint in the way which makes you the most money. You will minimize your meetings,* you will all *speak faster. You will only discuss in* meetings *things which help you make money* and where the use of Meatspace is the ONLY *way of getting the work done.*" He pauses for breath.

"I guess you can easily see why I say in the New World you must stop communicating."

The Global Communicator seems to find his tongue. "You cannot be serious. You cannot be suggesting that we stop communicating to our people. How will they learn about what the organization is trying to achieve?"

"Great question. We try to help people to learn by talking or writing **at** them. Or at best by talking and writing **to** them, and yet we know that *most people learn best by doing.* So why don't we communicate through the actual actions? Why don't we simply present the problem vaguely and allow people to get to work in delivering the results. Is it really true that people in an organization are completely paralyzed, immobile and un-moveable until they have had a mission statement communicated to them? A mission statement which covers all the organization's aspirations? Or perhaps there is another way. *Identify the stakeholders, give them little information, enough though to get started on actions and then and only then communicate with them at the right level of detail, at the right time using a medium which echoes the message you are trying to get across.*" He pauses, waiting for comments. There is an eerie silence. He waits another moment and then presses on. "If you really need to move information around, think about..."

He draws up on the flip chart.

Think about two things, the emotional content and the need to interactively communicate to deliver the result. Now think about where this is best tackled, in Touchspace or in cyberspace?

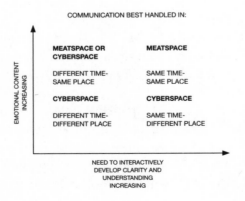

And now think about the best method. Don't forget, you must constantly strive to 'Move all constraints into Meatspace.' This means that you must make sure that all your interactions in cyberspace work 100%. You may need to invest resources and time to make sure that this happens.

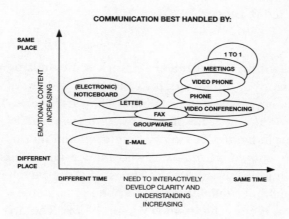

"I'd suggest five minutes, over coffee, no let's say fifteen minutes, for you to review how you personally and then your *organization makes use of cyberspace to support Meatspace.*"

Rule the Ninthe
Unlearn EVERYTHING!

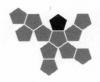

But remember, he said, that not being known doesn't stop the truth from being true.

R Bach

"Forget the Learning Organization." Franck commands provocatively. "Forget the learning organization as **the** goal. If there is a problem with *organizations, it is that they do learn*. They learn so well they stick to what they do rigidly. The problem with *organizations learning is that, unlike an individual learning, organizational learning happens in bits in the individual minds of the individual members of the organization*. It is all spread out. It's almost as if we each have a piece of a jigsaw, each piece is different and none of us know what pieces the others have if any. This creates two problems. The first is *actually getting the organization to learn the right things*. Checking what has been learnt across so many minds is now a near impossible task. It essentially means learning all the different things different individuals have learnt and then putting the whole picture together. In the Old World, the pace and effective use of experience meant that it was realistically possible to, over several decades, gain an understanding of how the bits fitted together. Secondly, *if the organization wishes to re-learn or learn something new it has to be implanted in different forms across the organization*. Of course, I must remind you that most organizations reward individuals for gathering and harboring the learning relevant to their job. Have you ever made a presentation to your senior management? I can bet that you prepared more slides than you intended to show. You had several in reserve just in case you were asked for other History Lessons or for further Fairy Tales? Usually, the people in the organization are encouraged to demonstrate that they possess vast numbers of Fairy Tales or History Lessons. And then, to make sure they don't forget or lose the answers they've learnt, we put in procedures and systems to capture and retain the learning. Not surprising then that trying to encourage people to give up and throw away such learning is an emotional bridge too far.

My slogan is *'Create Organizational Amnesia'*. You want your organization to see things for the first time, through a child's eyes each time. There is only one small problem, the reason why it is a slogan. Do you want to know why?"

A dozen heads nod.

"I don't know how to create **organizational** amnesia. I can do it myself but not to an organization. I use two methods. The first is that I *actively practice forgetting I know how to do things just so that I can make them up, from scratch, each time*. To achieve this you need to come to terms with the belief that you don't need to know all, if any, of the answers. Also you must believe *that it is OK to forget all your past successes*. If you are the sort of person whose confidence only comes from knowing what you have achieved, this method won't work for you. The second method I use is *to role-play someone else. I imagine myself to be someone who wouldn't know anything about the situation and try to figure out what questions they would ask and how they might feel*. Both approaches help me actively unlearn. Operating this way is very time consuming and wasteful but the results are worth it..."

Every Group a Culture

"I guess that the other reason why unlearning is important, is because of its impact on organizational culture. Have you ever thought about how a culture develops?"

There's no response.

"Lets go for a regional or national culture, I mean the culture of the Eskimos or of desert dwellers in the Gobi?"

"I think I read or heard something about the culture helping them to adapt to their environment. Not really sure," suggests the Self-Directed Team Leader.

"A lot of current thinking assumes *that cultures are simply collections of group habits and shortcuts*. The group realizes that the best way to survive in the desert is to wake up early and send the men off, in large Self-Directed teams, to look for food and water. As a result, a culture of rising early and traveling builds up as well as one which ensures that whilst the menfolk are away their other halves are looked after and kept away from any other menfolk (otherwise no-one will volunteer to go on the long walk in search of food and water). Voila! A culture.

Behaviors that support, encouraged. Behaviors that get in the way of survival, discouraged. Make sense?"

"Obvious when you describe it that way," comments the Process Re-engineer.

"You or I learn something, it's useful. Then we repeat it over and over. Now it's a habit. Now, we can be really effective because we can do without thinking. The speed and efficiency we gain benefits our survival. We're pre-programed. We can respond without thinking. I think when a group of people share the same unconscious programming of their minds, we observe it as a culture. Tell me, in the Old World how diverse were the activities and objectives of the organization?"

There is a silence. The answer is so obvious, the participants think Franck is trying to trick them into a trap. Franck runs round the side of the room to the back, puts his hand up, as if he is now a participant and answers his own question.

"Not very diverse," he replies.

Now he runs back to the front of the room and looking intense asks, "How many cultures would you recommend for an Old World organization operating in the Old World?"

Again he runs to the back of the room and puts his hand up to reply. This time the point is made and he has to answer through peals of laughter. "I guess in the Old World you would want one organizational culture and you would want it to be pretty strong, to guide and focus everyone on a particular recipe, aimed at a particular way of doing things."

This time he walks back to the front.

"Tell me, in the New World, how long are the customers satisfied with what you offer them?

This time the Self Starter replies, "Last night we heard that customers weren't happy very long and that their needs were different."

"So you have one customer segment who value speed of response and another who value the personal touch. Can you satisfy both through the same internal culture? Er, I don't think so. An internal culture geared around speed is likely to be incompatible with one geared around the personal touch. There may be some overlap *but if* you have a strong culture geared for one segment you can expect to upset the other segment."

"Are you saying that we shouldn't have a company culture?" asks the Empowering Manager.

"No. I think *as long as things are repeated, a culture will evolve,* but I'm suggesting that you do your best to modify it. *Try to replace a single culture with a common culture.*" Franck turns to the Strategic Program Implementer. "You've worked on projects? Have you noticed that the atmosphere on a project can be entirely different from one project to another?"

"Yes," replies the Implementer.

"Why is that?"

After a momentary pause the Implementer replies, "I guess *the purpose of the project has a big effect on the ground rules people work to.*"

"Can you explain a bit more?" requests Franck.

"Well, a bit like you said. After a while the project team sort of builds its own 'culture', it's a way of working which helps them towards their particular goals, cost focus, or specification focus or whatever."

"Absolutely!" He exclaims in support. "*You create a common culture and,*" he says, stressing the words, "*try to make sure that every team or group develops a culture appropriate to its goals.*" If you want to accelerate the process you run the same process in parallel at an organizational and at a team level. Work from either the objectives 'And!' from people's bad experiences of a similar activity to a set of ground rules. He distributes a handout entitled, 'Creating group habits'. It says:

CREATING GROUP HABITS

Step 1   Discuss which behaviours would help towards the objectives.

Step 2   Discuss which behaviours will get in the way of achieving the objectives (alternatively this can be done as a 'hopes and fears' exercise).

Step 3   Get agreement to the ground rules, behaviour (and thinking) best able to help the group.

Step 4   Look out for any breach, however minor, of the ground rules.

Step 5   Emphasise the breach and pounce on it hard.

Step 6   Look for any behaviour aligned with the ground rules and find every opportunity to praise the behaviour.

Step 7   Review the ground rules frequently reminding people of their existence and making absolutely sure that the ground rules are still appropriate for what you are trying to achieve.

Step 8   Keep looping round and you'll create a culture.

"Move on?"

There is unanimous agreement.

Only learn what others don't know!

"We've made a terrible mistake, we've told people that *they need to learn and to be innovative*. But we forgot to tell not to take us literally. A while ago we had a nightmare. We took on a team member who insisted on learning everything first hand, by doing. As a result s/he left a trail of devastation and errors in activities which previously had operated like clockwork. S/he resolutely refused to ask any advice or for any demonstrations by anyone else. When asked about his/her behavior s/he answered, "I thought I needed to learn." True s/he did, but not always first hand, a little second hand learning would have saved us a lot of time and resource, and secondly, *all that s/he was learning the group already knew the answers to. So the group did not benefit from all the work s/he did learning.*

Learning first hand, through trial and error, what others in your team or organization already know is a total waste of time. You see, *learning and innovating are not always the right thing to do. Just as not all change is improvement, not all learning develops the group's capabilities. In order to develop the group's capabilities you must focus on learning what others don't know.* And, just as not all learning is good, not all innovation is useful. In fact *innovation is useless unless the innovation is an improvement*. Should we look at one more rule before we have a coffee break?"

Rule the Tenf
DON'T CHANGE ANYTHING!

If you always do what you've always done you'll always get what you've always got.

"I first came across this quote about three years ago. When it was presented, it had everyone nodding. I nodded too and then, Bang! It hit me between the eyes. It's not true! The main reason we are all struggling with coping with the New World environment is precisely because we are always doing what we've always done. The problem is that we **don't** get what we've always got. *You see, the quote assumes that the environment is static and it is only your actions which represent change.* This, of course, is nonsense in the New World. Also we already know, *'change is not the same as improvement'*, and that *'learning what others already know is not useful'*. But there are other strong patterns. Other ways in which we can look at change. I call these, in order to make them look scientifically impressive, The Laws of Change." He displays a transparency:

Beware the Laws of Change

The First Law	One change leads to another.[30]
The Second Law	Adding change to change creates chaos.[31]
The Third Law	People create change – people constrain change. [32]
The Fouth Law	Accomplished change is change chosen and carried out carefully.[33]
The Fifth Law	The challenge of creating change is the converse of the accumulated complacency.[34]
The Sixth Law	Resistance to change accumulates over time. And the accumulated need for change can't be carried out all at once.[35]
The Seventh Law	Sparsely coupling change creates calm[36, 37]

"Have you come across these before?" he asks.

Five or six of the participants nod vigorously.

"Good, so I don't have to spend too much time on them. The first law is simply a warning. Remember if not all is improvement and you change something which isn't an improvement you will have to do more work to try to retrieve the money you lost on the first change. *'Don't change anything!'* is actually trying to force you into considering the implications of your change and then to fully justify them before altering anything. (In that way it is similar to *'Do nothing which is of no use!'*) And, it is trying to highlight the fact that the businessphere is constantly changing anyway. You may be able to take advantage of emerging situations but on the other hand if you change things you could lose these opportunities.

The second law highlights the need to pace the change. Again if at all possible, *'Don't change anything!'*

The third law concentrates on how human beings respond to change. Have you noticed how you always love your own ideas and yet don't get fired up by everyone else's or at worst treat them with total and utter contempt (unless of course they are similar to something you yourself had been thinking)?" Suddenly he looks pointedly at the gold and white clock at the back of the room and says flatly, "You know I said we would look at one more topic before the coffee break? We're going to have to skip the coffee break altogether this afternoon." He interjects, "And I think we're going to overrun by a couple of hours." Suddenly his face breaks into a beam of a smile. "Just kidding. How did you feel when I changed things on you unexpectedly?" he asks.

"We knew you were lying," replies the Informatized Manager.

"OK. But in that millisecond before you guessed I was making it up, did your stomach tighten slightly, perhaps a twinge of anger or uncertainty? That's what I'm interested in. You see, human design means that we interpret change, any change, as something threatening us. We first respond emotionally and then, and only then, if we're really lucky, the logic circuits kick in and we either try to rationalize it or work out how to make the best of it. If the logic circuits don't kick in, we just stay in the emotional state and try to resist the unexpected change. Have you ever heard someone else remind you of something that they said a year ago which they still stick to?" He stresses the words 'someone else'. "Do you think that they could have been actively or passively resisting change for the past year?"

He leans forward and looks accusingly in turn at each of the participants. Most of them are smiling guiltily.

"You see how long the emotional state can last? It's this very natural reaction that the third law is referring to. You see, if you invent the change yourself the instinctive reaction of resistance doesn't occur. Hence people create change and they constrain change.

Resistance to change is a resistance to any sort of change, improvement or not. By carrying out too much change, you may have switched everyone in your organization into an emotional state. Once people are reacting to you emotionally, logic and reasoned argument cuts no ice. If you have been surprising your people with lots and lots of change, you may already have made it impossible to change anything. *'Don't change anything!' is trying to keep the levels of resistance low."*

Proact and React

"*'Don't change anything!'* If you must, forget about doing things which are a direct extrapolation of what you are currently doing. In a New World environment, extrapolation is usually the wrong answer.

One of the most over-claimed quotes about how to cope with the chaotic, unpredictable New World environment is, *'The best way to predict the future is to create it.'* It's a great quotation. Direct, repeatable and, unless you take time to think about it, obviously correct. I wish I'd said it. I think it was first used by John Sculley at Apple. Recently when I made that statement I had three people contradict me. Each with their own candidate, so I guess we'll just have to assume it belongs to the ever prolific Anon. To effectively create the future you need to use two approaches simultaneously. *'Proact and react, don't extrapolate'*. He puts up a slide to illustrate what he is suggesting:

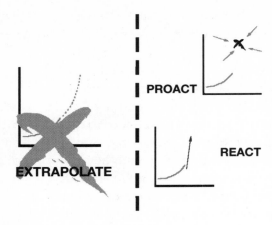

"Extrapolation is dead... long live?"

Seize the Future, Now!

"How good are you at imagining the future? *Being proactive is about anticipating the future and then putting in place activities which will influence it.* Last night we discussed the importance of future echoes. Proactivity where the future is obvious is a great way to make sure that that future actually happens."

Respond with Awesome Velocity

"One of the best slogans I have ever heard for reacting to the ever-changing business environment was from a Telecoms Company. One of the employees came up with the expression that they should *'move with awesome velocity'*. I agree but also apply the rules, *'Do Nothing...,* *'Don't change anything!'* and also *'Re-invent your information'*. Re-inventing your information will mean that you quickly use all four types of information so that when you see an issue and act, your awesome velocity creates a future you **really** want."

Robust or Bust!

'Don't change anything!' is also an effective rule for keeping your head. Because of the pressures of the New World and its apparent demands for continuous change it is *essential that you re-examine your personal values to check that they are robust*. What do you believe in? Are your beliefs still valid in spite of the turbulence? If you believe that people should spend time together, how does that survive the massive growth and take-over of Virtual Space World? I think you can try resisting the tide but I think you will lose. A far more robust belief would be that people should truly care for each other. Believing that people should truly care for each other transcends **how** they do it. Whether they write each other daily love e-mails or travel thousands of miles to spend time in each other's Touchspace. *'Don't change anything!'* is encouraging you to re-examine your beliefs to see which are robust. Trying to live your life through beliefs which are not robust, causes far too much stress and misery. *Trying to live with beliefs which are not robust means having to work far too hard to meet them. **Robust or bust** is how I describe that."*

The group is silent.

Franck realizes that he has crossed the unmarked border, the boundary between what people think is acceptable in a work environment and the discussion about what really matters, the feelings, dreams and wishes of individuals. He senses this, but doesn't care. He presses on. "By now you should know yourselves quite well. I'm going to ask you on your own to write down, draw, whatever, five things you would **never do** and five things you would **always strive to do**."

One participant asks for clarification, ten seconds later they are all deep in thought.

"Now I would like you, for each thing, to write along side it, Why. Why you would never do, etcetera…"

"Now check each one and see if it holds true, without trying to swim against the tide in both the Old and New World environments and in Here and Now Space and Virtual Space." Another period of time elapses. "Has anyone discovered anything that they are willing to share in public?"

The Global Communicator responds, "I've noticed two things. *My belief that life should be enjoyable and my belief that we shouldn't lie* *to each other, because lying is just cowardice by another name, hold up in **both** Old and New World, probably even slightly **more important** in New World.* But my belief that the only way to com-municate in business is face-to-face is likely to take a bashing. I guess you're right. The face-to-face thing contains an assumption on **How**. Really, all I really want to do in business communication is to demonstrate that I can be trusted and to check that the other person is willing to trust me, and vice versa."

"I had the same thing, well similar," adds the Self-Directed Team Leader. S/he then proceeds to explain. Over the next five minutes all the participants have shared their innermost beliefs. Franck is thinking, 'So much for off-limits topics.' *The New World forces us to examine our beliefs and values to make them more spiritual.* To spend more time with ourselves. For this you need to make time.

"*'Robust or bust'* helps to keep you from inner turmoil. But it's also a great approach for testing out strategies. Think about it, your orga- nization has developed a strategy, if that strategy isn't robust, it will either fail in the New World or it will need constant tinkering with. To test the robustness of the strategy play it against the fullest range of scenarios possible. What you are looking for is *a strategy which is still a good idea over a wide range of situations, rather than a strategy which performs brilliantly over a small range of situations and badly other- wise. Robust strategies require less maintenance and although they may not maximize your returns on paper, in reality they will provide a return. Kick off the strategy, planning not to 'change anything!'*"

Rule the Elevnf
LOOP IT UP!

To win without fighting is best

Sun Tzu

"There is a quote, I think it's from one of the contemporary business gurus, that goes *'the future is unknowable'*. I'm not so sure."

"I don't understand" states the Strategist, obviously perplexed by Franck's statement. "I thought that you had spent the whole morning telling us about the New World and how complex it was and how unpredictable it all was."

Franck smiles enigmatically and also too smugly, "Patterns!" he states without any real explanation.

"Patterns?" repeats the Strategist.

"Yes, patterns. Complex environments, like the chaos of New World, often have underlying, although complex and often non-repeating, patterns. If you can understand and spot the pattern you gain an insight into the future."

"Give me an example," insists the Strategist.

"We all know that most of the time strategies attempted in the New World fail. One reason, we discussed, is because of the assumption we named *'fair = equal'*. We know that in many situations applying this thinking means that we under-emphasize the importance of the bulk of the players in a situation. Net result: under performance. We don't adjust our approach to meet the requirements of the actual situation." The Strategist nods, half convinced. Franck seizes upon this neutral reaction to return to his hypothesis. "Chaos has patterns. Many people think of chaos as random. New World isn't random. It is the result of millions of interlocking cause-and-effect loops. Let me walk you round one so that you can begin to see the underlying structure. These days most people are worried about the uncertainty in the business world. They worry if they will keep their jobs. One person, let's call hem Bobby is so worried that when s/he receives his Xmas bonus of £300 s/he is in no doubt at all about what to do with it. What do you think s/he does with it?"

"I don't know," replies the Strategist flatly.

"S/he saves it. S/he invests it. S/he puts it into hes pension fund. What do you think happens next?"

"S/he regrets it?" the Strategist suggests with little commitment, betraying that s/he is unsure of the right answer.

Franck chuckles, "Probably. Because guess what the pension company does with the money?"

"No idea."

"Who owns most of the companies in the world?"

"Pension funds," comes back the answer.

"So the pension fund decides to buy shares in a company with the £500 investment. If all they do is buy the shares, the share price will rise faster than profitability and as a result the returns will fall. So any pension fund, with any muscle worth its while, will inform the board of their intention to purchase the shares of their company." He pauses and looks round the room to make sure everyone is following his story. "Guess what happens next?"

"They buy the shares?"

"Yes, but not before the board is aware of the pressures put on them to improve profitability. Now as the tale unfolds, unfortunately the fund buys shares in the company Bobby works for. I know you are thinking 'Why unfortunately?' Because the board of Bobby's company frantically looks round for ways to raise the profitability in order to meet the increased target returns. They look for ways to do it, spot Bobby in hes role, think, 'Well there's a saving we could make'. Bobby is fired instantly and it's all hes own fault for saving that extra £500."

The group erupt in laughter at the simplicity of it.

"So guess what happens next? At Christmas time Bobby's colleague Eric receives hes bonus. Eric is feeling particularly insecure because of the sudden departure of Bobby. Eric decides..." The group erupt into laughter again.

"The reason it seems so funny is because it is inevitable. That, and the fact that it sort of loops back on itself. It feeds itself. What amuses you is the phenomena of increasing returns. With increasing returns if the outcome is good we describe it as a virtuous cycle. If the outcome is bad we refer to it as a vicious cycle. It means that safety is not the safety of one day nor is danger the danger of one day. Both safety and danger come from gradual development." He puts up a hand-written slide and runs his pen as a pointer along the arrows in the picture. First along the arrows in the loop and then along the arrows hanging off the loop and finally along the arrows resulting from the loop.

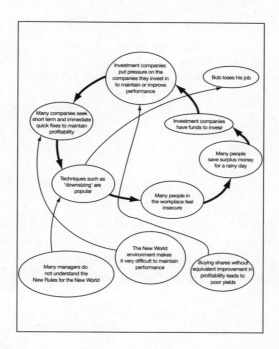

"The trick," he says, his voice lowered in tone and volume, rolling his 'r' in almost Gaelic pronunciation, "the trick," he repeats, "is to build your own loops and set them to work for you. The other trick," this time he grins, "is to break every single loop that is negative, and to break it fast. In the New World a year is a long time and you may never recover if you let a negative loop last too long."

There is a hushed silence. All the group look intensely pensive. He asks, "Should we move on?"

Form Loops

"Forming loops is not easy, thinking through how the loop should operate is easier. The type of loop most people are keenest on is a money making loop. A money making loop is brilliant because it grows whilst it keeps on making you money." He draws:

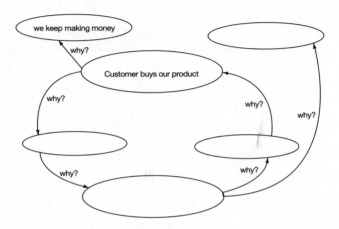

"If you can find the answers to fill those bubbles you're doing very well. Then, to *make sure that your loop keeps going you need to ground it with anchors.* Grounded loops are brilliant because they usually withstand changes in the businessphere. They obey '*Robust or bust!'*

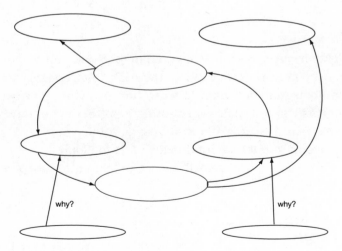

You've probably noticed that it's also very similar to the diagram I showed you on interdependence." He walks to the flipchart and turns backward about a dozen pages. "Of course it is. The *interdependence*

you desire *is* also *co-evolutionary*. Once in a loop, it's very difficult to get out. So, just a word of warning, be really careful who you decide to include in your loop. What happens if you choose a customer segment for your loop, whose businesses are struggling or who have less and less spending power? What happens if you let someone into your team who is evil? I use the word metaphorically but, **don't put in the team anyone you wouldn't leave your kids with**. You won't ever achieve interdependence, or if you do, you'll wish you hadn't." He grins a wicked grin.

Break Loops

"In the New World, because many people don't understand the New Rules, they find themselves trapped in loops, vicious cycles which go on and on round and round. For example, people who don't understand *'Make time Fit!'* will complain about a lack of time which leads to an inability to reflect, which in turn leads to fire-fighting which leads to a lack of time. Seeking and breaking loops always releases the motivation and resource you need to create new virtuous loops. The technique is relatively simple. It's literally three steps."

1   *Draw the loop and anchors.*
2   *Choose two bubbles on the loop to reverse.*
3   *Choose one or more of the anchors, root drivers, to eliminate.*

"Last night we talked about the obnoxious customer who was forcing your margins down. Why don't we work in buzz groups to solve that one?"

Rule the Twelf
GO VIRTUAL!

> *A dog at a PC, sending an e-mail to another dog. The e-mail says, "On the internet, no one knows you're a dog".*
>
> Anon

"What do telephone banking, television, car hire and call diversion have in common? To anyone in Touchspace, they can't tell the difference between what they are expecting in Touchspace and what they actually experience. They are virtual activities, having the effect of the traditional output without the traditional form. The latest I came across was a virtual pet, which creates a mess on the living room carpet, makes affectionate noises if you touch it and dies (stops working) if you ignore it."

"You're kidding," says the Empowering Manager incredulously.

"No it's true," Franck replies crossing his heart. "There is nothing completely new about virtual activities and products. Cinema was one of the first virtual products and not surprisingly the organizational structure that cinema created, of projects (films), teams(crews), individuals (stars), core processes (marketing), resource managers (agents) and so on is being actively emulated by successful organizations today. The real difference is that New World and Virtual space give us a whole new range of opportunities, especially in internal organizational activities and customer service offers."

"What do you mean?" asks the Re-engineer.

"OK, let's look at an example of an internal organizational activity."

He pauses scratching his forehead for an example, "Erm, one of you was late arriving last night?" He is trying to remember who looked flushed and hot at the first evening session.

"That was me," confesses the Global Communicator.

"You were very good, you phoned ahead to let us know. Isn't that right?"

"Yes I left a message. Yes, two. When I got closer I lost my bearings and got a bit lost. I spoke to your receptionist about it and asked for directions. She was very good. I must say I was surprised that she was still in the office so late."

Franck grins his wicked grin and says, "You've been here all day and been all round the building haven't you?"

"Yes."

"Where does the receptionist sit?"

The Global Communicator starts to answer and then his jaw drops leaving his lips slightly parted, "I don't know." He finally manages to utter in bewilderment. "I haven't seen a receptionist. Is there a basement?"

"No." replies Franck pointedly. "You haven't seen a receptionist because there isn't one. Your calls didn't come here, they went some-where else. They went to another company which specializes in taking other people's phone calls. **They** gave you the directions, not us."

"What about my messages?"

"They came through here electronically seconds after you left them."

"And where is the lady who took the call?"

"I haven't the faintest idea," replies Franck. "Could be anywhere. The important part of the discussion is that *you received the service you were expecting, but it didn't have the traditional form. And you didn't even know. It was a virtual reception.* I'm coming to believe that there is no internal or external offer which can't be made virtual in some way. *Every activity OFF the money making process should be made virtual. And activities ON the money making process should also be made virtual, but activities which are core to future money making should be carried out by the core members of the organization so that the four types of information can be gathered first hand.*"

"I see what you are saying. Making something virtual is simply a case of finding a different way to reach the same outcome."

Franck points at his nose saying, "On the button, better than I could I have said." Now he turns to the Global Communicator and asks tentatively, "How come you thought we had a receptionist here?"

"I guess because that is the norm. That and the fact that I dialed your number. When you dial a land line you think that the phone which rings is at the number you are dialing. You almost have a picture in your mind of the phone on the person's desk and them picking it up. That and, I guess, because the receptionist was so good at giving me directions, I didn't think to question."

"Thanks, that was a perfect answer."

Copy Everyone, Imitate No-one

"By far the best gift that *'Go virtual!'* gives us is that it eliminates some of the uncertainty of the New World. It eliminates a lot of the risk involved in innovation. If you can *find new ways of delivering old needs* you already know who the customers are, where they are and what color underpants they wear. It's all out there for the taking but the real barrier is in your imagination. You see, to be able to *'Go virtual!'* you will need to redraw your mental maps. We need to *build new mental maps.*"

Don't Eat the Menu!

"In our minds or hearts we have a model of what we think is happening every time we do anything. *'Go virtual!'* challenges all those models, the mental maps, the emotional gut feelings and the images we carry around with us to help us make sense of things. We all know that the menu isn't the meal but it is good enough to give us the information we need to decide what the actual experience will be like. Sometimes, as well as or instead of the menu, we have a picture of the meal, and in Japan it is common to have the meal itself displayed. But that is also a model. The real problem for those of us in business is that we accept the models as long as they match reality. But what happens when reality changes? Don't forget that not being known doesn't stop the truth from being true." He waits for an answer.

"I guess we need to change the models?" shrugs the Empowering Manager.

"But most people don't know about New World or understand about Virtual Space. Let me show you one of the most popular models we use in strategy." He quickly sketches:

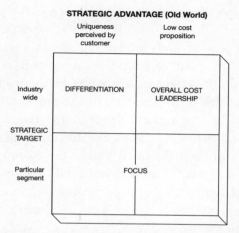

And yet we know when we look around us that products are constantly being launched and launched. In some areas product launch is one big *'And!'* Like frogspawn, if we produce enough, quickly and cheaply enough, some will grow up to be frogs and perhaps someday be kissed by a princess. In other areas we make something so delightful, tasty and fulfilling, with a lovely aroma that anyone coming across it wishes to sample its delights. We are *fair* to them *by providing* something *different*. In other areas we look to build relationships, grow and develop with our customers and suppliers. We *build* them into our *loops*.

All three are valid New World routes to strategic advantage. All three are virtual, they allow us to gain strategic advantage without the traditional approach."

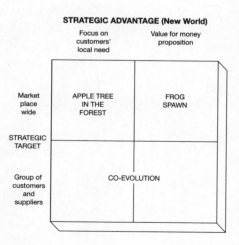

In the Old World, we would warn organizations of the perils of getting 'stuck-in-the-middle'. Being stuck in the middle meant that you lost all the sources of strategic advantage and gained none. We assumed a big 'Or'. We assumed that organizations must focus on one approach or another. But that thinking was right. Efficiency meant that focusing on one route was the best. Also, organizations would tend to have single measurement and reward approaches, and a single way in which 'we do things around here'. So the thinking was definitely right. The menu matched the meal. But in the New World? Perhaps we could apply an *'And!'*. Perhaps you could co-evolve with some customers, whilst apple-treeing a particular segment, whilst at the same time deluging the market with a range of other offers?"

He waits for comment.

"Perhaps you could use all three sources of advantage on different offers, provided you made sure that you didn't confuse the people in your organization. By ensuring that *'every group has an appropriate culture'*, the organization could, if it wanted, leverage all these sources of advantage at the same time."

"Doesn't what you're suggesting require a high level of sophistication and discipline?" challenges the Strategist.

"Perhaps. But what would you do, if it was your own money, in the New World?" Franck's question hangs in the air. No-one answers.

Pressing the Start Button

Unlocking Your Potential

... don't forget what you did today. It is easy to forget our times of knowing to think that they've been dreams...

Richard Bach

"So you really want to move to the New World. All the earlier sections have considered the theory, mind-sets and emotional commitment you need to survive and thrive in the New World. I have some very bad news for you. All we've covered so far is completely pointless, a waste of time."

The real problem is that none of it works without YOU. Nothing works without **YOU** changing **YOUR THINKING** and **YOUR BEHAVIOR**. All the theory suggests that changing your thinking is tough, but doable. The real nightmare is changing your behavior. I bet you won't. I bet you will want to, you may even try some of the New World behaviors we've discussed here for a week and the more determined of you for a month. But eventually you'll give in, your old habits will win. Depressing, isn't it?"

The Self-Directed Team Leader protests, "I'm sure we'll do much better than you suggest."

"Mmm perhaps. I am a real pessimist I suppose. I can only look at myself. I find it really hard to change. You have probably learnt some new behaviors as an adult; your golf swing, changing nappies, driving a car. And yet the real difficulty is altering the way you do these things. Once you have learnt to drive, you tend to remember to brake but changing your habit of braking too sharply is difficult. You can swing the club but you keep twisting your wrist. And so on."

Franck receives support from the Re-engineer. "Yes," s/he says, "changing is really tough and there isn't enough time to really get into the change when you are under pressure."

"I guess if you're having trouble with time you need to use the fourth and sixth rules, *'Do Nothing...'* and *'Make time fit'*." Franck is teasing them. I guess you've got to realise that *the time you give it is the same as all the time you have to give to changing*. It's all you get, so *'Do Nothing...'* insists that we get as much out of it as possible." He grins. "All we have to establish is that you **do** have a choice in **your** future. So we'll use this last session to help you think through what you need to do to become a New World Manager."

He changes tack, he says, "Have you ever tried to change something about yourself before and succeeded?"

"There are a few 'Yeses'

"Tried and failed?"

A louder chorus.

Franck hands out packs of yellow sticky notes and says, "Please write, one for each note, the things which helped you to succeed or fail. Once you're done please stick them on this wall," he says pointing to the back wall. "Please try to stick your sticky close to ones with a similar theme. Ten minutes?"

Now the yellow pieces of paper cover the back wall. Four main groupings are apparent, with a sprinkling of half a dozen rogue stickies not grouped. Franck stands near the wall reading them. "This group seems to be about **motivation or insight**, this one about **objectives or vision**, this one seems to be about **ability/skills/know-how**, and this group over here is something to do with **environment or context**. Great!" he says with masses of positive energy. He returns to the front of the room and bullet points them on the flipchart.

- *insight and motivation*
- *objectives and vision*
- *ability/skills or knowhow*
- *environment/context*

He fills in the headings along the top and turns it into a table.

Franck says, "You need to fill it in for your own use. I'll tell you what, why don't you as a group fill this flip chart version in collectively. Meanwhile I'll get some individual copies made." He leaves the room.

Factor	Enabler	Enabler Helper	Blocker	Blocker Buster
• Insight and motivation	• • •	• • •	• • •	• • •
• Objectives and Vision	• • •	• • •	• • •	• • • •
• Ability/ skills or know-how	• • •	• • •	• • •	• • •
• Environment/ , context	• • •	• • •	• • •	• • •

Date today: /   /   Date of next Review: /   /

When Franck returns a quarter of an hour later, the table is full of writing.

Factor	Enabler	Enabler Helper	Blocker	Blocker Buster
• Insight and motivation	• Feedback • Reviews of progress	• Seek feedback from others • *'Make time fit!'* for reviews	• Fear of failure • Fear of success • Lack of insight	• Remind yourself of situations where you have been courageous • Imagine the success not disrupting what you have already achieved
• Objectives and Vision	• *'Communicate purpose'* • Explore your feelings	• Draw pictures on paper or in your mind • Describe it to a third party • Explore how you will feel as a result	• Lack of examples • Not taking time to visualise • Going for the default option	• Read widely • Discuss with friends and share experiences • Spend more time with Franck
• Ability/ skills or know-how	• Don't know how to apply the skill • Reward yourself for improvements in applying the skill • Get information about progress and success	• Rehearse in your mind • Read a book called *New Rules for the New World* • *'Loop it up!'* • *'Reinvent your information'*	• Old habits – new action similar to old • No mentor • Fear that existing jobs/ tasks will suffer	• *'Unlearn everything'* • Find challenge • *'And!'*
• Environ-ment/ context	• Redefine your environment, move, change jobs • Meet new people	• Change work/ home environment • Change the 'gang' you hang out with	• Money	• *'Fair = different'*

Now he hands out a blank matrix, an empty table for them to complete individually. They complete box by box the matrix. A matrix of wishes, a matrix of tasks and tricks, a matrix to grow them into the New World.

The room is completely silent. Silent for what seems an age. Then slowly the conversation started as a trickle and then a flood. Now the conversations are punctuated by random peals of laughter. Throughout, Franck has been standing motionless at the front of the room, eyes fixed on the back wall.

The Merged Chief Executive asks, "How do we know which role to use rule to use when?"

He seems to spring back to life. "You can think, or you can guess or you can use luck."

"Luck?" repeats the Self-Directed Team Leader.

"Yes, luck." Now he picks up a final handout. This one is in colour. There is a green, almost human shape, like a strange dancer, made up of regular geometric units.

"Turn this into a 'dice'," he advises. "Roll it if you need to decide which New Rule to apply. You'll find it always gives you the right answer."

"Is it a magic dice?" asks the Strategist.

"No," replies Franck, grinning. It's just a 'New World dice'."

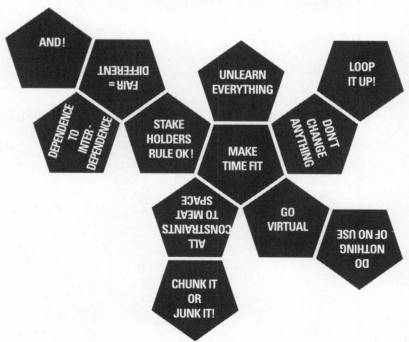

"I guess that's it guys." Franck announces. "I guess all I can do now is wish you Good Luck. He moves towards the Self-directed team leader and shakes his hand with warmth. He says something, but his words are lost to the group who also, by now, are shaking hands, patting each other on the back and gathering up the spiritual energy and emotional resilience to return to the New World.

The Jargon Section

Who knows?
Who understands?
Who cares?

Anon

Accountability
Accountability is linked to tasks (not resources as it is often misused), as in, *'You can count on me to deliver this task, process or project'*. Accountability usually resides with a single individual although if **interdependence** is evident, a team (but never a network) can also be accountable

Business environment, Businessphere
This term is used to describe the external conditions within which an organization has to operate. It includes pressures such as the number of competitors; the amount and quality of legislation generated by Government; and the interest and attitude of consumers. All these aspects influence the choice of best actions an organization must make to achieve its goals.

Capability
As in *capable*. It describes the organization's ownership or access to the people, knowledge and physical resources which make it capable of carrying out activities.

Change Projects
These are internal **projects**. They are driven by the organization which has to change.

Client/Client Organization/Consumer/Customer
The Client/Client Organization/Consumer/Customer is the person or organization which wants to use the output or **offering** from a **money making process** or **project**.

Closed Projects

Closed **projects** have clear goals and a clearly defined set of activities to be carried out. In general, there is clarity about WHAT is to be done and HOW it is to be carried out. They are often characterized by the phrase 'we will know when we have completed the clearly defined deliverable'. Examples include building a bridge or launching a clearly specified new product. Colloquially described as **painting by numbers**.

Core Team

This consists of the sub-group of people who are completely committed to the goals of the **process** or **project** and have a high level of **inter-dependence**. Often they will be able to commit their time to the activities and have skills or expertise essential to delivery of the offering.

Culture

Culture consists of two fundamental elements:
1. The norms and behaviors of a group, i.e. 'The way we do things around here.'
2. Unconscious programming of the mind leading to a set of *similar collective assumptions, habits, behaviors and* **mind-sets**.

Deliberate Strategy

See Directional Strategy.

Dependence

A form of interactivity where one action or person acts as a **precursor** or **prerequisite** for another action or person. **Dependence** often operates on a scale from Nil to 100%.

Directional Strategy

A directional **strategy** is a statement of 'where we want to go'. It has clear goals and the way forward is clear. There is little uncertainty so forward planning is appropriate.

Emergent Strategy

An emergent **strategy** is one which is continuously evolving. It is characterized by loosely defined goals and uncertainty about how to proceed. It involves rapid **Plan-do-Review cycles**.

Typical emergent strategies often appear to be statements of 'how we got here.' Examples include implementing culture change programs and realigning business processes with customer demands. In both cases it is easier to define "what we don't want to be" than "what we do want to be".

Flock
Flock is the word used to describe a group of specific chunks of change, **projects**, which make up a **program**. They are *loosely coupled but tightly aligned*.

Fog Project/Foggy project/Walking in the Fog/Foggy Change
When referred to in formal terms, such **projects** are described as **open**. This type of project occurs when you are unsure of both WHAT is to be done and HOW it is to be done.

Going on a Quest
See Quest **Projects.**

Hard Objectives
These define the measurable aspects of what the **process** or **project** will deliver. Typically they include the *time, cost, specification and terms and conditions.*

Illegitimate Change/Illegitimate Projects/Change not Improvement
Changes or **Projects** which do nothing to help the organization reach its goals. A change which does not contribute to the current or future profitability of an organization or any of its other goals. Pet projects, out-of-date projects where business needs have changed since the project was set up fall into this category.

Independence
People or activities which can achieve their goals without relying on any other inputs or resources as **precursors** or **prerequisites**.

Investment
The money an organization spends on goods/services and information it intends to sell and all the money it spends on skills, knowledge and equipment to give it the **capabilities** it needs to generate money.

Interdependence
A form of interactivity where one action or person acts as a **precursor** or **prerequisite** for one or more actions or people who in turn act as precursors or prerequisites for the initial action or person. And if you don't think that that is a load of mind-twisting gobbledegook, you're a genius. The real problem in understanding interdependence, is that many people don't. However, it is by far *the most essential of the least well-understood concepts of effective team working.* Interdependence means that a team member cannot succeed unless the other members also succeed.

Improvement/Legitimate Change/Legitimate Project
A **change** or **project** which contributes directly to the goals or an organization in terms of current or future real revenue or **throughput**, **operating expense** or **investment**.

Mind-set
Useful but rather demeaning management professional's short hand expression for the set of assumptions, rules and perceptions people carry around in their heads. It implies fixed content and an inability to learn.

Money making loop
The magical loop which grows money. The money making loop is a set of dependent activities or events by customers and suppliers which lead to the constant flow of money from the customer to the supplier simultaneously with the constant flow of delight and useful- ness from the supplier to the customer. A good money-making loop is a **dynamically stable co-evolutionary** set of activities. This is the cause-effect relationship which generates the business revenues. Anchored by **core drivers** a money making loop can persist in an organization for decades. Within the complexity and chaos of the organization's structure, markets and so on, the money making loop acts as a strange attractor. Money making loops are essential to prolonged business prosperity.

Money making process

The primary **process** in a business organization. This is made up of all the activities required day-to-day to change inputs into offerings for which the customer will pay money.

Movie Project (Making a Movie)

Formally a **semi-open** project. **Projects** where the means are known but the objective is unclear.

Network

A group of people who are interconnected through knowledge of each other and often through one or more communications medium or forums. Occasionally they will share a common goal simultaneously but often they will operate by exchanging information or resources to support each individual in their own goals.

New World (also see Real World)

New World refers to a set of conditions which determine that the business environment behaves in a complex and chaotic manner. New World is associated with business environments where organizations actively pursue change, are global in terms of competition and make use of information in order to ensure that most communication to customers, suppliers and employees is very fast, global and accurate. These organizations operate in activities where competition is intense and customer expectations arising from this competition continuously spiral out of control. In such industries the convergence of technologies makes the emergence of new, non-traditional competitors commonplace whilst at the same time the businesses need to use a wider and wider range of skills, competences and technologies to produce and deliver their offerings, making the business more and more difficult to directly manage. The people working in businesses expect to be empowered and to contribute to the decision making and business operational process. The intellectual as well as physical contribution of the members of a business to all its activities is paramount.

In general, the rules for business success in New World are very different from the rules for success in more static business environments.

Old World (See also the World before Midnight)

Old World refers to the business environment where command and control hierarchies provided the best route to delivering business results. The business environment was largely predictable and mass market approaches were still effective. People working for organizations expected to be un-empowered and quite looked forward to that.

Open Change/Open Projects (Also see Fog Projects, Movie Projects, Quest Projects)

Open **projects** have loosely defined goals or unclear means. The general direction is understood but the end point is hard to identify. They can be characterized by the statement 'we will get closer than we are'. Examples include implementing transformation programs, and investing in pure scientific research.

Operating Expense

The running cost of the business; all the money that the business spends to produce goods or services it intends to sell – usually equivalent to fixed costs.

Operating Expense Rate

The rate at which you need to spend money in order to run a business.

Plan-Do-Review

A plan-do-review cycle involves planning a small step to try something out, completing the step and reviewing progress to see what has been learnt before planning the next step.

Process

A process is a "river of change".

Processes create change though simultaneous or near simultaneous activities upon materials, people or information. Activities stay roughly the same day-to-day, however the medium passing through the activities is altered.

Processes are described by either the end objective (e.g. money making) or the method employed (customer marketing).

(Also see money making processes, core or secondary processes.)

Process Manager

The person accountable and responsible for managing the process. Ensuring effective management of constrained resources, the output meets the **hard** and **soft** objectives, process team morale, providing information of the effectiveness of the process to the team and to other **stakeholders**.

Project

A project is a "chunk of change".

It is an effective way of creating change through a sequence of activities which occur through time. Activities often include: the definition of project objectives by reconciling the objectives of a diverse group of **stakeholders**, then planning, coordinating and implementing the activities necessary to achieve these objectives to the satisfaction of the stakeholder group. (Also see **process**).

Objectives

These spell out what a process, project or program is trying to achieve in terms of **hard** objectives and **soft** objectives.

Project Leadership

Project leadership is the discipline of leading and managing projects. Leading the visible and invisible teams to achieve the objectives of the **stakeholders**.

Project Leader

The project leader is the person who is **accountable** for getting the project completed.

Project Portfolio (See also Flock)

The group of projects which are managed by a strategic project leader or **program** manager. Each project in the portfolio (**flock**) contributes to the achievement of the overall strategy.

Quest Projects (Going on a Quest)

Going on a Quest is formally known as a semi-open **project**. You are clear of what is to be done but clueless about the means.

Real Revenue Rate
The rate at which an organization generates money through sales less real variable costs.

Real World (also see New World)
A less emotive way than "New World" of describing the current business environment of most industries today. It encompasses change, discontinuity and a real reliance on the intellectual as well as physical contribution of members of a business.

Responsibility
Responsibility for the *use of or access to resources* is a key aspect of any New World organization. It is essential that organizational **capability** is maintained and this role is aimed at achieving just that.

Smart Delegation
Smart delegation is about each person delegating to another stakeholder all/any tasks which the other **stakeholder** is more competent or powerful to perform (See subsidiarity)

Soft Objectives
These relate to how the change should be managed in terms of relationships. Typical soft objectives include how the project should be controlled, how communications are to take place, what to do in case of emergencies. A project-specific soft objective might be, 'This is very sensitive information, we don't want it widely known'.

Stakeholder
A stakeholder is anyone who has an interest in the project. A typical project has some stakeholders who support it and some who oppose it. A useful way to identify stakeholders is to ask, "Who is impacted by what this project is trying to achieve?" And then to produce a stakeholder map.

Typically key stakeholders are:
- people you need as resources
- people you need to take along
- people who are going to be affected by your change
- people on the sidelines who are watching the progress of the change.

Stakeholder Map
A useful way to understand the relationships between the **stakeholders** is to draw a map.

Strange Attractor
In non-linear systems there is a capability for the system to demonstrate behavior which is within bounds but unpredictable. Such behavior is termed chaotic. A strange attractor is the name given to the stable center of such systems.

Strategy
Conscious manipulation of the future. This is a **New World** definition. In the New World organizations acknowledge the futility of detailed long range plans and concentrate instead on visions, frameworks, multiple, overlapping and co-evolving change activities, infrastructure platforms and rolling plans. The intention is to try over time to create the future you have invented before.

Old World strategy was a form of linear planning at worst or at best an attempt to 'fit' resources to the environment or the problem. **New World strategy** acknowledges the *multi-dimensional, non-linear* nature of the business environment and defines strategy as 'Conscious manipulation of the future'.

Strategic Implementation
Concurrent manipulation of a range of changes designed to:
- identify and establish constraints to current/future business performance
- define and discover the gaps between the current reality and the future vision
- decide on the source of future constraints and designing control and co-ordination systems and measurements
- defining problem set or objectives to be addressed by strategic **program**

Strategic Project Leader
Strategic **project** leaders act as the conduit between those who formulate strategy and those who implement it on the ground, the project leaders. To be effective in this role they have to understand

how **strategy** is formulated and the problems faced by their project leaders. In addition, they need *leadership and process consultancy skills*.

Typically a strategic project leader has a project portfolio, flock, and acts as the sponsor for each project in the portfolio. Reconciling conflicts between projects, setting priorities, elements of the strategic project leader's job.

Subsidiarity
(see smart delegation)

Supplier Organization
Supplier organizations are all those suppliers and subcontractors, external to the project organization, who provide the goods and services which are required for the project to be completed.

Team
A group of people with a common **goal**, a recognition that to achieve that goal and to achieve success, they are **interdependent** and a willingness to take personal **accountability** for the activities which need to be carried out.

Throughput
The rate at which an organization generates actual money through sales. (See revenue rate.)

Virtual
To have the effect without the traditional form (e.g. Virtual reality has the effect of reality without actually being real).

Virtual team
Any group which has the effect of being a team without the traditional trappings, e.g. co-location, single leader, etc.

Virtual organization
An organization which uses the range of **capabilities** and enablers available to deliver offerings using non traditional form.

World before Midnight (Also see Old World)

This describes the business environment before the full impact of the chaotic, information based, change dominated current business environment.

Books to read if you get a chance!

Below is a list of books which either:
a) helped me with my thinking and frameworks as I researched and developed this book, or
b) acted as a counterbalance of Old World thinking and helped me to express my thoughts better.
You have to guess which is which and then decide which ones I'm recommending you read.

Achieving Organizational Magic!, Eddie Obeng, 1997

All Change!, Eddie Obeng, Financial Times Pitman, 1996

At Home in the Universe, Stuart Kaufman, Viking, 1995

Being Digital, Nicholas Negroponte, Hodder & Stoughton, 1995

The Canterbury Tales, Geoffrey Chaucer tr. Neville Coghill, Cresset Press, 1992

The Canterbury Tales Illustrated Prologue, Geoffrey Chaucer ed. Michael Alexander, Scala Books, 1996

Creating Tomorrow's Organization, David Birchall and Lyons, FT Pitman, 1996

Competitive Strategy, Michael Porter, Free Press, 1980

Complexity, M.M. Waldrop, Penguin 1992

Fad Surfing in the Boardroom, Eileen Shapiro, Capstone, 1997

The Fifth Discipline, Peter M. Senge, Century, 1990

The Haystack Syndrome, Eliyahu Goldratt, North River Press, 1990

Key Management Ideas, Stuart Crainer, Financial Times Pitman, 1996

The Machine that Changed the World, James P. Womack et al, Rawson Associates, 1990

Making Re-engineering Happen, Eddie Obeng and Stuart Crainer, Financial Times Pitman, 1996

Out of Control, Kevin Kelly, Fourth Estate, 1994

Putting Strategy to Work, Eddie Obeng, Financial Times Pitman, 1996

Teleworking, Steven Burch, Kogan Page, 1991

Corporate Man to Corporate Skunk, Stuart Crainer, Capstone, 1997

Virtual Community, Howard Rhiengold, Secker & Warburg, 1994

The Virtual Corporation, William Davidow ans Michael Malone, Harper Collins, 1996

The Free Cut-out

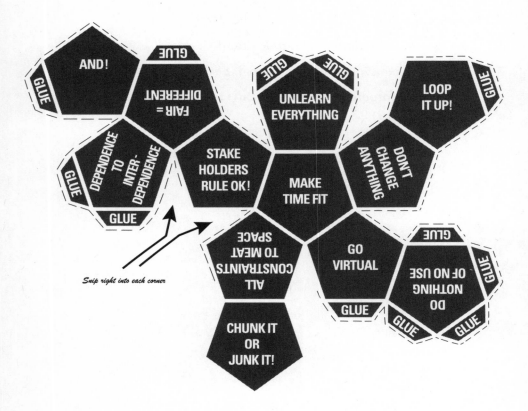

AND!

GLUE

FAIR = DIFFERENT

GLUE

UNLEARN EVERYTHING

GLUE

LOOP IT UP!

GLUE

DEPENDENCE TO INTER-DEPENDENCE

GLUE

GLUE

STAKE HOLDERS RULE OK!

MAKE TIME FIT

DON'T CHANGE ANYTHING

ALL CONSTRAINTS TO MEAT SPACE

GO VIRTUAL

GLUE

DO NOTHING OF NO USE

GLUE

GLUE

GLUE

GLUE

CHUNK IT OR JUNK IT!

Snip right into each corner

FREE

New Rules selection dice

When to use: are you looking for inspiration or ideas on how to achieve a breakthrough? Simply roll the New Rules dice to discover what to do next. Or roll the dice anyway.

Instructions for assembly

1 Cut out the shape. Then use the scissors to snip right up to any corners.
2 Crease along all white gaps by folding each section back on itself.
3 Apply glue to flaps.
4 Fold and attach flaps. Try not to get sticky glue all over your fingers.
5 Roll dice.

Notes on the Text

1   I'm assuming that you know what the 'New World' is. If you don't, you can either read the summary in the Old World/New World discussion in the section after the acknowledgements or you can read *Achieving Organizational Magic!* or *Making Re-engineering Happen*, both of which spend significant time explaining the concept.

2   From *Making Re-engineering Happen*, Eddie Obeng, Financial Times Pitman, 1995.

3   See the Second and Third Laws of Change, from *All Change!* Financial Times Pitman, 1996. The Second Law states that adding change to change creates chaos.

4   Meatspace/Touchspace is the environment which physical matter and atoms and creatures such as you or I inhabit. I prefer the term Touchspace to Meatspace. However Franck tends to use the word Meatspace in his section of the book.

5   Cyberspace is the environment inhabited by bits and digital data. For example whilst I was writing this book on Olive Oyle, my brown Olivetti Echos 48 notebook computer, I only printed it out when it was complete. So for the bulk of the time it only existed in cyberspace.

6   Meatspace is the environment which physical matter and atoms and creatures such as you or I inhabit.

7   See New Rules Applied section Paradox busting – And!

8   See New Rules Applied section. You are not alone.

9   The Third Law of Change is explained fully in *All Change!* Eddie Obeng, Financial Times Pitman, 1995. Simply stated as: People create change – People constrain change. The Law warns against imposed solutions.

10   See New Rules Applied section on Money-making machines.

11   See New Rules Applied section You are not alone!

12   See New Rules Applied section on Money-making machines.

13   See New Rules Applied section You are not alone!

14   See New Rules Applied section on Paradox busting.

15   See New Rules Applied section on Paradox busting.

16   I define Strategy as the conscious manipulation of the future. A strategic problem is a problem, which if left to fester has significant implications for the foreseeable future.

17   See New Rules Applied section on Information and Communication.

18   See either the Prologue section on Old World/New World or for a full explanation see *Making Re-engineering Happen*, Eddie Obeng, Financial Times Pitman, 1995.

19   See New Rules Applied Section 6 on Time also Unlocking your potential – Creating time.

20   The full discussion of the impact of New World on time is presented in Chapter 5 of *Making Re-engineering Happen*, Eddie Obeng, Financial Times Pitman 1995.

21   From *Achieving Organizational Magic!* Eddie Obeng, 1997.

22   See section on Old World/New World for brief explanation.

23   See section titled Go Virtual.

24   See the Empowering Manager's Tale.

25   See The Business Benchmarker's Tale.

26   See The Tale of the Change Implementer, the comments about the Regulator.

27   See *All Change! The Project Leader's Secret Handbook*, Eddie Obeng, Financial Times Pitman, 1996.

28   From *Achieving Organizational Magic!* Eddie Obeng, 1997.

29   *Complexity*, M.M. Waldrop, Penguin, 1992.

30   Further reading in *All Change! The Project Leader's Secret Handbook*, Eddie Obeng, Financial Times Pitman, 1996.

31   Further explanation in *The Fifth Discipline*, P. Senge, and *All Change!* Eddie Obeng.

32   Further explanation in *All Change! The Project Leader's Secret Handbook*, Eddie Obeng, Financial Times Pitman, 1996.

33   Further explanation in *All Change! The Project Leader's Secret Handbook*, Eddie Obeng, Financial Times Pitman, 1996.

34   Further explanation in *Making Re-engineering Happen*, Eddie Obeng and Stuart Crainer, Financial Times Pitman, 1996.

35   Further explanation in *Putting Strategy to Work*, Eddie Obeng, Financial Times Pitman, 1996.

36   Further explanation in *Achieving Organizational Magic!* Eddie Obeng, 1997.

37   Further explanation in *At Home in the Universe*, Stuart Kaufman.

Index